Behold Your Little Ones

Edited by

Barbara B. Smith and Shirley W. Thomas

BOOKCRAFT
Salt Lake City, Utah

Library of Congress Catalog Card Number: 99-72222

ISBN 1-57008-620-6

First Printing, 1999

Printed in the United States of America

If these are the last days,
and all things are to be gathered in one,
and we are in truth the forerunners
of the second coming of our Lord and Savior Jesus Christ,
what a vast responsibility rests upon us!

—BRIGHAM YOUNG JR.

Contents

Preface

$\mathcal{T}$O BE THE FORERUNNERS AS CHRIST'S coming draws nearer may well be the opportunity of the generation of children born into this the Saturday night of time. Surely it is a period of special challenge, quite aptly called a "night." We do not know how long the night will be, but whether these children are making ready for the resurrected Lord to actually come, in His clouds of glory, or for them to be received by Him into an eternal reward, the preparation they need is the same. Wondering how parents, grandparents, friends, and family might help to prepare and support these "Forerunners of Christ," we conceived the idea of this volume of collected essays.

In developing an outline, we could think of no better source of instruction for preparing to meet the Savior than His own words. We found in the record of His visit to the Nephite people that much of His concern was for the well-being of children and families. We appreciate Sister Colleen Maxwell, Elder Neal A. Maxwell's wife, and her tenderness toward little children, as we see it in her approach to these passages: "In 3 Nephi 26:14 we read, 'and it came to pass that he did teach and minister unto the children of the multitude . . . and he did loose their tongues, and they did speak unto their fathers great and marvelous things, even greater than he had revealed unto the people; and he loosed their tongues that they could utter.' What powerful imagery! How blessed were those children!"[1]

The scriptural topics for the fourteen chapters of this book are from His teachings, found in the pages of 3 Nephi. A dozen able women joined us in writing the chapters, each one bringing a

valuable point of view and each having been honed by rich experience. Their pieces vary widely but are uniformly useful and freshly
appealing.

Among the last of the Savior's directives to the Nephites in His
three-day visit was His insistent "All thy children shall be taught of
the Lord" (3 Nephi 22:13). While the programs of the Church provide remarkable instructional opportunities for children, Christ in
teaching the people emphasized the way learning in the home com-
plements the teaching offered in the Church. After hours of giving
information and explaining doctrine, He stopped and said, "I perceive that ye are weak, that ye cannot understand all my words . . .
at this time. . . . Therefore, go ye unto your homes, and ponder . . .
ask of the Father" (3 Nephi 17:2–3). Our book opens with a focus on
this scripture and on the role of the home as a place for study and
learning. Ensuing chapters each consider a different facet of life. Each
is based on a teaching of the Savior as it relates to the family, with particular concern for the spiritual needs of a child—and, as important,
the spiritual needs of adults as they relate to children.

This spiritual necessity for "grown-ups" to have the example little
children provide was made clear in Christ's teachings. Here is a relevant account shared by Sister Maxwell: "An admired scripture scholar
was discussing in a small group how frequently the scriptures
admonish us to become as little children. Having such a love of little
children, I went to the scriptures to reaffirm that powerful notion.
Some of these stirring scriptures mention many qualities that are so
evident in children. We are strongly told that unless we are converted
and become as a little child, we shall not enter the kingdom of
heaven. And again, that if we humble ourselves as a little child, 'the
same is greatest in the kingdom of heaven' (Matthew 18:4)."[2]

In keeping with our need to understand little children (in order
to become as they are), chapter 2, "Behold Your Little Ones" (3 Nephi
17:23), looks at the spiritual nature of a child. Next is a discussion of
what it means to be "of the covenant" (3 Nephi 20:25), and how to
help a child know this. Then the happy topics "His countenance did
smile upon them" (3 Nephi 19:25), "Be of good cheer" (3 Nephi
1:13), and "Blessed are you if ye have no disputations among you" (3
Nephi 18:34) follow in sequence, each one turning to the Light as

they do a different quality of a little child. A change of tone comes with "And the winds blew, and beat upon that house " (3 Nephi 14:27), followed with "But my kindness shall not depart from thee" (3 Nephi 22:10).

The next pages contain the lighthearted "Then shall they break forth into joy" (3 Nephi 20:34) and "With the voice together shall they sing" (3 Nephi 20:32), and the family-unifying "Hold up your light that it may shine" (3 Nephi 18:24), giving emphasis to family goals and emblems. "Great shall be the peace of thy children" (3 Nephi 22:13) holds a beautiful promise, whereas "Become as a little child" (3 Nephi 11:37) is a more serious challenge in which we become both learner and teacher, helping a child understand himself as we learn from him.

The last chapter of the book deals with the culminating promise of the Lord: "Then shall the power of heaven come down among them; and I also will be in the midst" (3 Nephi 21:25), emphasizing that the Lord will assuredly come in a glorious hour that no man may know, bringing heaven with Him. In addition, when we can create a heavenlike place here, in our homes and our gathering places, and when we are on His errand, then we may feel His power and presence (see 3 Nephi 21:25).

We recognize that this volume is small in the large scheme of the Lord's work and is not a publication of the Church. But we hope that it finds a place in the hearts of those who, as we do, delight in finding new insights into beloved gospel themes or who may be pleased to learn of effective ways to heighten family experiences, and especially those who care for and care about little children. Sister Maxwell's words are appropriate: "Knowing how precious they are to their Heavenly Father and to our Savior, how imperative it is that we protect and love them and keep them unspotted from the world so they can fulfill their promised destiny—that of being 'sanctified through the atonement' (D&C 74:7)."[3]

Finally, we express the privilege it has been to work with the outstanding women who have written the chapters that comprise this book, each one an example of what she writes.

Barbara B Smith

Shirley W. Thomas

NOTES

1. Colleen H. Maxwell, unpublished typescript in authors' possession.
2. Ibid.
3. Ibid.

CHAPTER ONE

A Learning Place ✓

"Go ye unto your homes, and ponder . . .
and ask of the Father."
—3 NEPHI 17:3

by
Sydney Smith Reynolds

We have the responsibility to make our homes a gospel learning center where the scriptures, the doctrines, and the teachings of the prophets are taken seriously. Our doing so will bless our children with a strong core of values that will provide a basis from which they will be able to operate successfully when they meet the world.

"Parents have a sacred duty to rear their children in love and righteousness, to provide for their physical and spiritual needs, to teach them to love and serve one another, to observe the commandments of God and to be law-abiding citizens wherever they live."

THE FAMILY: A PROCLAMATION TO THE WORLD

*W*HEN THE SAVIOR SAW THAT THE Nephites could not understand all the words He had spoken to them, He instructed them, "Go . . . unto your homes and ponder" (3 Nephi 17:3) upon the things He had told them. His admonition ascribes to our homes a beautiful function as a place for learning and understanding sacred things. In our homes we have an invaluable center for gospel learning. It is the place where we learn to pray, where we learn what faith is, where we come to listen to the whisperings of the Spirit and feel the Lord's guidance in our lives. Our homes are also the place where we learn from our childhood days the importance of learning itself, how to learn, and the value of seeking an education.

In the Doctrine and Covenants the Lord gives a commandment that we should "teach one another the doctrine of the kingdom." He said, "Teach ye diligently and my grace shall attend you, that you may be instructed more perfectly in theory, in principle, in doctrine, in the law of the gospel, in all things that pertain unto the kingdom of God, that are expedient for you to understand" (D&C 88:77–78). Certainly this applies to parents in the home.

Children learn to pray in their homes as they are invited to say their evening and morning prayers, ask a blessing on the food, and take a turn in family prayer. They learn the importance of prayer as they watch their parents pray over their fields, their employment, their children, and their daily bread. Noel Reynolds wrote: "The child's belief and understanding of the divine is shaped in his early years, especially as he observes how the divine shapes the important

SYDNEY SMITH REYNOLDS and her husband, Noel, are the parents of eleven children and reside in Orem, Utah. Sister Reynolds holds a bachelor's degree from Brigham Young University and enjoys taking classes to further her study. She is currently a member of the Primary General Board and, as part of that calling, writes the Sharing Time page for The Friend *magazine.*

actions of his parents. The farm boy who sees his father dedicate the fields to God every spring has no doubt whence come the rains. But when his father talks about God only on Sunday, as it were, and then conducts his life's business as if Chance ruled the universe, the child may very well learn to farm like an atheist."[1]

The daily habit of prayer is reinforced in those difficult times when the family gathers and its members pour out their hearts to the Lord for a loved one who is ill or out of work or in need of some other special blessing. Elder Jeffrey R. Holland recounted an experience he had as a young boy of five or six years. His grandfather was seriously ill and the family had assembled for prayer. Elder Holland was the only non-adult present but he was invited to be a part of that prayer circle, which included many of his family members as well as the stake patriarch. Each person took a turn praying out loud and, lastly, it was his turn. He recalled: "I had participated in family prayer, the blessing on the food, bedtime prayers, and the other prayers that children say, but I had never experienced prayer like this before. . . . The patriarch later told me that he felt my grandfather had been healed primarily because of my prayer. I have never forgotten that experience. . . . Prayer took on a deeper meaning for me."[2]

This personal experience enhances our appreciation for Elder Holland's warning in a general conference address about the short-sightedness of giving our youth a "kind of theological Twinkie—spiritually empty calories" which can feed but not nourish.[3]

Today's parents have been alerted to the importance of studying nutrition labels and providing the basic food groups for their growing children. They assume their children will learn their ABCs, master mathematics, and become computer literate. Though prayer is one of the first things children will learn in our homes, we should remember that one of the most pointed messages to parents in the modern scriptures recounts our responsibility for doctrinal teaching in the home: "Inasmuch as parents have children in Zion, or in any of her stakes which are organized, that teach them not to understand the doctrine of repentance, faith in Christ the Son of the living God, and of baptism and the gift of the Holy Ghost by the laying on of the hands, when eight years old, the sin be upon the heads of the parents" (D&C 68:25).

We have the responsibility to make our homes a gospel learning center where the scriptures, the doctrines, and the teachings of the prophets are taken seriously. Our doing so will bless our children with a strong core of values that will provide a basis from which they will be able to operate successfully when they meet the world. This is not a church that isolates in a monastery, out of the world, those striving for perfection. Our homes provide a haven from the world, but they should also help prepare our children to understand, meet, and influence for good their brothers and sisters throughout the world.

Where and how does this teaching take place? Obviously in the home, and primarily by example. Primary leaders tell a story about a boy who could always tell where his mother had been in the house when he arrived home because her scriptures would be there open.

Another story was told many years ago of a prominent family in the Church who were known for their doctrinal knowledge. A friend asked the father how they had all come to be such scripturalists, so well versed in doctrine. "I give credit to the Sunday School program for that development," replied the father.

"Oh, really," remarked his friend. "That hasn't exactly been my experience with Sunday School classes."

"Now, don't mistake me," replied the father. "When we came to Sunday dinner, I asked the children what they had learned in Sunday School that day. We spent the next hour and a half discussing and setting matters straight."

Whether or not such a story is apocryphal, it gives some guidance as to possibilities accessible to all of us.

Family home evening is another educational opportunity. Children usually keep coming to family home evening if parents care enough to convene it and treats are provided. One friend revealed that she finally got the picture about family home evening. "We used never to have it, because I felt like I didn't have any pictures, or games, or other fabulous activity planned. I thought to myself that I'd get it ready for the next Monday, but too often the same thing happened. I'm glad I finally figured out that the most important thing is to have it." Her insight is a valid one. Few specific lessons will be memorable in the long run, but the cumulative effect of regular gospel instruction and meeting together at the prophet's direction cannot help but be felt.

We can never warn our children against every specific evil they may encounter in this life, nor should we try. What we can do is help them become familiar with the Holy Spirit themselves. Then they will have a voice of warning or counsel, a bad feeling or a good feeling, whenever they need it. If they keep the commandments and learn to hear the voice of the Spirit, they can weather any storm.

And it's obvious that this generation will have storms to face. In the verse following that quoted earlier in this chapter the Lord charges us to learn about "things both in heaven and in the earth, and under the earth; things which have been, things which are, things which must shortly come to pass; things which are at home, things which are abroad; the wars and the perplexities of the nations, and the judgments which are on the land; and a knowledge also of countries and of kingdoms" (D&C 88:79). This all-encompassing list would gladden the heart of any high school academic counselor or university general education advocate.

What is the responsibility of parents in encouraging this kind of education in their homes? A spate of articles in the popular press has underscored the importance of the home environment and those who care for infants. At stake are brain development and a child's ongoing ability to learn. An article in *Time* magazine related recent discoveries of neuroscience labs and concluded that "deprived of a stimulating environment, a child's brain suffers. Researchers at Baylor College of Medicine . . . have found that children who don't play much or are rarely touched develop brains 20 to 30 percent smaller than normal for their age."[4]

Other studies suggest that an infant's neural connections laid down by repeated sensory experience provide the basis for learning math, music, language, and so forth in later years. A *Newsweek* article dated February 19, 1996 talks about "time limits" or "critical periods" which are "windows of opportunity that nature flings open, starting before birth, and then slams shut, one by one, with every additional candle on the child's birthday cake." The study cites an experiment on a newborn kitten who had one eye sewed shut. "So few neurons connected from the shut eye to the visual cortex that the animal was blind even after its eye was reopened. Such [blindness] did not occur in adult cats whose eyes were shut."5

These studies address not only physiological stimuli but also emotional patterns that develop in children as parents reinforce a child's exclamations of joy or of wonder and help them deal positively with pain or disappointment.

All of this has profound implications for parents and policy makers and justifies concerns about leaving the very young in the care of others. As the *Time* reporter said, the data "underscore the importance of hands-on parenting, of finding the time to cuddle a baby, talk with a toddler and provide infants with stimulating experiences."6 Parents are almost always best suited to provide such nurturing.

In 1998 as electioneering got under way, the public press reported a backlash attitude against earlier "politically correct" notions. Women who were seeking public office and yet had very young children, or were expecting, found themselves facing serious opposition to the idea that they should be running. A new attitude in the land seemed to be that the very best public service a woman could be engaged in was to nurture her own children in the first years of their lives.

In a proclamation to the world, the Church has declared: "Parents have a sacred duty to rear their children in love and righteousness, to provide for their physical and spiritual needs, to teach them to love and serve one another, to observe the commandments of God and to be law-abiding citizens wherever they live."7

Home is the principal place to learn such things. Another important thing we learn in the home is just how important learning and education are. Virginia Noel was the middle child in a family of fourteen children who grew up on a farm in Vernal, Utah, during the Depression. Her mother wrote poetry in her very limited spare time. Her father had come west with a brother who had asthma and made his own way as a ranch hand, trading post operator, and civil clerk. There were educational values in this family, but times were hard and pursuing an education took determination and grit. Virginia had both. After high school she worked hard raising turkeys her father had obtained for her. Having made ten dollars, with the money she bought a suitcase and a new hairbrush; and pocketing the remainder she was off to the Agricultural College in Logan to become an elementary schoolteacher.

She worked her way through school, graduated, and started teaching school in Vernal. She met and married a wonderful man who had dropped out of high school to help support his family after the death of his mother. Because of his service in World War II he was eligible for a homestead in Wyoming, and the little family moved up there to conquer the sagebrush. There was lots of work, no running water, no electricity for years, and very little money. But there were trips to the library, the purchase of a piano, and the expectation that English would be properly spoken. The children in that family report being bilingual—they spoke "cowboy" and, thanks to their mother, they also spoke English. In the first generation all seven children attended college. They have between them two Ph.Ds, two J.Ds, an MBA, and countless books, travel experiences, and musical instruments. Their healthy respect for the value of growing up on a farm was enhanced by their mother's encouragement to raise their intellectual horizon above the haystack.

My own grandfather, Thomas D. Rees, was first a school superintendent and then a medical doctor. Education was an important value for him. His two sons both pursued higher degrees: one was an M.D. and the other a Ph.D. But his daughters remember him saying, "If I had to make a choice between sending a son to school or sending a daughter, I'd send the daughter." A woman's education, he believed, impacted the whole family and future generations even in ways that a man's did not. Both of his daughters graduated from university in a day when few women sought the opportunity of attending. Both have reared families where education is valued.

Does valuing education mean that we all need to pursue formal schooling through the Ph.D. level and beyond? Of course not. Learning is a lifelong process. In good schools, as in good homes, one not only learns but also learns how to learn and to appreciate learning. The most educated people are those who have never stopped learning.

A case in point is Mary Craig Thompson. Mary Craig emigrated from Scotland when she was four years old. The family settled in Australia when it was still quite an adventure just to be there. To help her family financially she had to go to work after the equivalent of eighth grade. All her life to that point she had eaten oatmeal for breakfast. Once she was contributing to the family income she didn't have to eat oatmeal any more. She never ate it again for the rest of her life.

But though she was delighted to give up the oatmeal, she could not bear to give up learning. She found work in Australia doing laundry and then as a cook and cleaning woman. She worked hard and she worked long hours, but she always found time to read. She joined The Church of Jesus Christ of Latter-day Saints and came to the United States. She traveled, she read, she listened, and she never stopped learning. She was a sought-after "literature" and then "cultural refinement" teacher in every Relief Society she entered. She joined book groups and was often invited to give reviews. She loved doing crossword puzzles and other word games. She kept abreast of political and cultural affairs and acted as a tour guide for friends in Europe and Australia. Because of her friendship with my mother, she was like a second mother to me and to my brothers and sisters. Her attitude toward education seconded my parents' similar attitude in valuable ways.

How do different families encourage learning and valuing education? There are many ways, but here are a few that recur with frequency when that question is asked.

Have books available. That can mean owning a critical number of books, making trips to the library as part of the normal schedule, accessing school libraries, and controlling the use of television and computer games.

Talk with your children about what you are reading, what you observe, what you both are learning from the newspaper or the TV. Help children understand what sources are reliable and how to discern worthwhile material from fluff and/or trash.

Travel when you have the opportunity. When you don't have the opportunity, invite others who have traveled to share their experiences with you and your family.

Enhance the learning environment of your home with books, works of art, good music, fine craftsmanship. Is there a place where you can read if you want to? Is there a quiet place to study or write? Parents are usually a major factor in a child's understanding of the importance of finishing a task, getting homework done on time, being responsible for helping around the house, developing self-discipline through music lessons or participation in athletics.

Teach the value of work and the skills of home management. Our grandmothers would be amazed that we would need to be reminded to teach something about nutrition, cooking, cleaning, mending, and nurturing children. Our grandfathers would be interested to know that children don't automatically know something about planting, weeding, mowing, and harvesting.

In a general conference address President Gordon B. Hinckley reminded parents: "It is not enough simply to provide food and shelter for the physical being. There is an equal responsibility to provide nourishment and direction to the spirit and the mind and the heart."[8]

What a blessing it is to parents and children when we take that admonition seriously and strive to make our homes a center for learning in a setting where love abounds!

Notes

1. Noel B. Reynolds, "Cultural Diversity in a Universal Church," in *Mormonism: A Faith for All Cultures* (Provo: BYU Press, 1978), p. 20.

2. Jeffrey R. Holland, "Friend to Friend," *The Friend,* August 1996, p. 6.

3. Jeffrey R. Holland, " 'A Teacher Come from God,'" *Ensign,* May 1998, p. 26.

4. J. Madeleine Nash, "Fertile Minds," *Time,* February 3, 1997, p. 51.

5. Sharon Begley, "Your Child's Brain," *Newsweek,* February 19, 1996, p. 56.

6. Nash, p. 51.

7. "The Family: A Proclamation to the World," published in 1995 by The Church of Jesus Christ of Latter-day Saints, paragraph 6.

8. Gordon B. Hinckley, "Bring Up a Child in the Way He Should Go," *Ensign,* November 1993, p. 59.

CHAPTER TWO

Children: A Loan from the Lord

"Behold your little ones. And as they looked
to behold they cast their eyes towards
heaven, and they saw the heavens open, and
they saw angels descending out of heaven as
it were in the midst of fire: and they came
down and encircled those little ones about,
and they were encircled about with fire; and
the angels did minister unto them."
—3 NEPHI 17:23–24

by

Elaine Hansen Hatch

*There are many times when we could be guided by the Spirit
if we would be but very still and listen. We could know how
special, how valuable our children are to God.*

"You will be startled . . . to realize how familiar the face of our Heavenly
Father is. But when you see him, you will know his voice, because you will
have prayed, listened, obeyed, and come to share the thoughts and intents
of his heart."

HENRY B. EYRING

---

*T*O "BEHOLD" CAN INDICATE A MUCH broader, a much deeper, and a more spiritual interpretation than is thought of at a casual glance. In *Webster's Dictionary for Everyday Use* "behold" means "to look at, to fix the eyes upon, to observe carefully."

These adult Nephites who were privileged to associate with Jesus Christ on His visit to the American continent must surely have beheld in wonder. Though they were "more righteous" than their compatriots who had been destroyed, they were still in great need of repentance (see 3 Nephi 9:13). That the Savior graciously condescended to come down into their midst and instruct them suggests that the repentance process was already beginning.

Apparently the children Jesus lovingly blessed and prayed for on that occasion had no such difficulty. They were "little children," "little ones" (3 Nephi 17:21, 23). Thus it is highly probable that they were all under eight years of age, therefore incapable of sin and needing no repentance (see D&C 29:46–47). Indeed, one cannot help wondering whether these children, many of them fresh from heaven, might have readily recognized the Savior from premortal contacts, thus giving credence to the tender and perhaps inspired words of the seventeenth-century poet Henry Vaughan in his poem "The Retreat."

 Happy these early days, when I
Shined in my Angel-infancy!
Before I understood this place
Appointed for my second race,
Or taught my soul to fancy aught

ELAINE HANSEN HATCH is a graduate of Brigham Young University and has taught school in Utah and Pennsylvania. She now serves on the board of trustees of Southern Virginia College and on the International Affairs Committee of the Church. She and her husband, Senator Orrin Hatch, are the parents of six children and have homes in Salt Lake City, Utah, and Vienna, Virginia.

But a white, celestial thought;
While yet I had not walked above
A mile or two from my first Love,
And looking back, at that short space
Could see a glimpse of His bright face.

As the parents beheld the marvelous event, they must have recognized that their children were even more beautiful, more excellent, more Christlike than they had realized. Their joy must have been consuming as they witnessed the magnificent spirits of these beloved children who had been entrusted to their care and teaching, observing them being taught and prayed for by the Savior Himself and by angels straight from heaven.

Clearly, the children were not afraid of anything that was taking place—not in any way fearful of Christ, or His angels, or the fire surrounding them. After this the children no doubt grew up as stalwarts in the faith, taught and nurtured by repentant parents who displayed gentleness, kindness, and love in their families. While we have not had their supernal experience, by diligent effort we too can be parents of this caliber. We too can have obedient, righteous children who will be the heralds of Christ. This should be our goal.

Elder Henry B. Eyring clarified even more our closeness to our Heavenly Father by quoting this statement from President Ezra Taft Benson: "Nothing is going to startle us more when we pass through the veil to the other side than to realize how well we know our Father and how familiar his face is to us." Elder Eyring amplified President Benson's statement by adding: "But when you see him, you will know his voice, because you will have prayed, listened, obeyed, and come to share the thoughts and intents of his heart."[1]

Abraham Lincoln once said, "All that I am or hope to be, I owe to my angel mother." Many of us could also say that, and we certainly hope our children will be happy to say that about us.

"Heavenly Father intended that each child should have the combined loving protection and guidance of caring parents. . . . The Christ child grew and developed in a modest home, where Joseph earned a humble living as a carpenter, and where Jesus also learned this craft. . . . The example of Joseph and Mary in providing a suitable home for their large family was such that Luke recorded that Jesus 'grew and waxed strong in spirit, filled with wisdom; and the grace of God was upon him.' . . . [By] teaching children before the age of accountability [parents can] dress them in armor in preparation for the battle against sin. Every child is entitled to live in a home, as Jesus did, where there is an environment permitting growth in gospel understanding."[2]

From the very beginning, man was assigned to be the provider and woman was assigned to be the nurturer. This is the way the Lord designed it.

"Decades of child development research show that what all young children need to grow up emotionally healthy is a warm, affectionate relationship with their mothers. I am not aware of any research indicating that a 'caregiver' is even an adequate long-term substitute for a mother, much less a good one."[3]

To the women of the Church, President Gordon B. Hinckley gave this counsel in the October 1996 general conference: "I hope that if you are employed full-time you are doing it to ensure that basic needs are met and not simply to indulge a taste for an elaborate home, fancy cars, and other luxuries. The greatest job that any mother will ever do will be in nurturing, teaching, lifting, encouraging and rearing her children in righteousness and truth. None other can adequately take her place. It is well-nigh impossible to be a full-time homemaker and a full-time employee."

From the White House Conference on Families in 1986 it was said, "For most . . . life is not a matter of legislative battles, judicial decrees and executive decisions. It *is* a fabric of: helping hands and good neighbors, bedtime stories and shared prayers, lovingly packed lunchboxes and household budget balancing, tears wiped away, a precious heritage passed along, hard work and a little put away for the future.

"In a healthy society, heroes are the men, women, and children who hold the world together one home at a time; the parents and grandparents who forgo pleasures, delay purchases, foreclose options and commit most of their lives to the noblest undertaking of citizenship; raising children who, resting on the shoulders of the previous generation, will see farther than we and reach higher."[4]

Mother is a child's lifeline. A house can be a terribly lonely place without a parent at home. Speaking to mothers, Elder H. Burke Peterson said: "There is a darkness that comes [into the home] when there is no mother there. Children are not a gift to us, but a precious loan, a priceless loan to be returned—returned more valuable than when we received them. . . . The charge is ours to increase their worth. . . . [God] created you to learn to be a good mother—an eternal mother. It is your first and foremost calling."[5]

If we can do this, earnestly strive to do this, we may have to miss some social outings, cut back on another obligation, and so on; but let us never mind that, because so much more will have been gained of what really counts in this life and in the eternal plan.

Sister Virginia Jensen, in an address to the women of the Church, said, "There are only a few . . . places in which our influence is irreplaceable. I can imagine children the world over saying, 'When you decide where to spend the time and the gifts that God has given you, Mom, choose me.' "[6]

The father is also vital in the home, helping to rear the children as well as providing a living for his family. The story is told of a young man who was to be sentenced to the penitentiary. The judge had known him from childhood and was well acquainted with his father, a famous legal scholar. "Do you remember your father?" asked the judge.

"I remember him well, your honor."

"As you are about to be sentenced and as you think of your wonderful dad, what do you remember most clearly about him?"

There was a pause. Then the judge received an unexpected answer. "I remember when I went to him for advice, he looked at me from the book he was writing and said: 'Run along, boy. I'm busy!' When I went to him for companionship, he turned me away, saying, 'Run along, son, this book must be finished!' Your honor, you remember him as a great lawyer. I remember him as a lost friend."

The judge muttered to himself: "Alas! Finished the book, but lost the boy."[7]

May we never lose sight of what is truly of value in life, what our purpose in life really is. What is of *eternal* worth? Fathers and mothers working together is the Lord's way.

Pablo Casals, the great cellist, once said: "We should say to our children, each one of them: Do you know what you are? You are a marvel. You are unique. In all of the world there is no other child exactly like you. In the millions of years that have passed there has never been another child like you. And look at your body—what a wonder it is! Your legs, your arms, your cunning fingers, the way you move! You may become a Shakespeare, a Michelangelo, a Beethoven. You have the capacity for anything."[8]

In a meeting for stake Relief Society presidents, Elaine Jack, former General Relief Society President, shared an idea given to her by Mary Ellen Edmunds. The latter suggested that when parents can't think of any other positive characteristic of their child at the moment, they could honestly compliment their adolescent, even if it was like this: "Son, you breathe really well. I like the way that you breathe, in and out, in and out, so regularly and nice."

"Behold Your Little Ones"
Behold them at play or in sports.
Behold them at school.
Behold them when they leave for school and when
     they come home.
Behold them at church.
Behold them with their friends.
Behold them at parties.
Behold them when they are alone.
Behold them in every situation you can.
     Be constantly aware.

While helping our daughter and her family move into a new home in a new city, I questioned her as to why the computer was set up in the family room rather than in the den or the library. She answered wisely: "In the family room we can keep track of what is happening. Other rooms in the house are off the beaten track and could eventually, but innocently, allow unsavory programs to be watched."

As we "behold our little ones," we have many protective "circles of angels" in our lives—home, temple, family home evening, family prayer, seminary, righteous friends, and so forth. These are havens from the storms. Let us touch on just a few of these.

FAMILY HOME EVENING

Members of the Church have been counseled for a long time to meet together as a family at least once a week and teach the gospel. This will have eternal consequences. In 1915 the First Presidency said: "If the Saints obey this counsel, we promise that great blessings will result. Love at home and obedience to parents will increase. Faith will be developed in the hearts of the youth of Israel, and they will gain power to combat the evil influences and temptations which beset them."9 This beautiful promise has been reiterated by all the prophets since it was given. It has never been withdrawn. It is a simple command, but let us not underestimate its power.

Several years ago we invited a few friends to our home for a dinner party. I learned a valuable lesson from one couple, who served at one of the temples on Friday evenings. Their reply to our invitation was: "We would love to come to your home, but if we let other things keep us away from our service that night, it all becomes very difficult. Soon we are finding a multitude of excuses not to be at our post. If we let nothing interfere, it is easy."

Could it be the same with family home evening? If we let nothing interfere and we hold it consistently every week, then family home evening is easy. But the day we let other activities or commitments infringe on that time, we are in essence robbing our families of great promises, closeness, and all else that binds a family together.

SCRIPTURE STUDY

Scripture study is another very simple thing we are asked to accomplish daily. "I feel certain" said President Marion G. Romney, "that if, in our homes, parents will read from the Book of Mormon prayerfully and regularly, both by themselves and with their children, the spirit of that great book will come to permeate our homes. . . . The spirit of reverence will increase; mutual respect and consideration for each other will grow. The spirit of contention will depart.

Parents will counsel their children in greater love and wisdom. Children will be more responsive and submissive to the counsel of their parents. Righteousness will increase. . . . The pure love of Christ will abound in our homes and lives, bringing in their wake peace, joy, and happiness."[10]

Doctrine and Covenants 6:12 counsels us, "Trifle not with sacred things." Our children along with our covenants are our sacred things. We must never take our children for granted and always keep our relationship with them sacred and honorable.

A beautiful promise from the Lord given to missionaries in earlier days may perhaps also help us along life's path: "I will go before your face. I will be on your right hand and on your left, and my Spirit shall be in your hearts, and mine angels round about you, to bear you up" (D&C 84:88). No doubt many of us have had experiences of this kind. They make us feel loved by and important to God. We also realize how important our help to Him is, especially as we "behold [our] little ones" and fulfill our stewardships as we help prepare them for the Lord's second coming.

BE SUPPORTIVE OF YOUR CHILDREN

Parents need to support their children in their activities. Children too have gifts and talents given them. Both at school and at church, many opportunities afford themselves—sports, music, concerts, debates, plays, and so on. Children often act as if it doesn't matter to them whether their parents are there. It may be many years later before parents realize that it did matter—a lot! A gentle, excited, even self-confident spirit perhaps was either encouraged or suppressed at that time.

In 1997 we celebrated the great westward movement of our pioneers. The Lord built a strong foundation for the Church in this dispensation. As the Saints crossed the plains, their children were right beside them. Children's responsibilities on that trek were often way beyond their years, but they were also strengthened and spiritually fortified, as were the adults, to be able to bear great burdens and to fulfill their destiny. Perhaps those children too were surrounded by angels and their burdens were lightened. As these parents beheld their little ones, how gratified, how thankful they must have been! At times they must have stood all amazed at the workings of the Spirit in those precious ones.

From these noble souls came people of strength, testimony, love, and purpose who have blessed the lives of us all and made it possible for the Lord to continue His plans.

WE BUILD FOR THE SECOND COMING

We today must build a strong, worthy foundation for the return of the Savior. This must be done home by home, family by family. Both buildings and organizations need strong, firm foundations in order to weather the storms of life.

As we behold our little ones, do we see in them who they really are and who they can become? Do we remember that they are God's sons and daughters? Do we recall our sacred stewardship to bring them back to the God who gave them life? Do we recognize their spiritual qualities?

Sister Carol Ann Nawracaj, a Bernadine Franciscan nun, in her tender book *Treasures from Heaven*, says she becomes overwhelmed in the presence of newborns because she feels she is in the presence of the sacred. She tells of a conversation with a preschooler about the birth of his new sister.

"When I congratulated him and asked how he felt about the baby, he replied, 'She's so small that I have to be real careful when I'm around her because I could accidentally hurt her. But I love to look at her and touch her, because she still has God's fingerprints on her.' "[11]

One wintry day when our own youngest son was six years old, he put on his winter togs and on his way outside announced, "I've got to go out and choose the right." That evening he informed us that he had shoveled the neighbor's driveway.

A grandmother tells the story of her little grandson wanting a picture of Jesus. They gave him the famous one of Christ with the little children. As he opened the anticipated package he started to cry. Between sobs he said: "No, it just isn't right. He holds us on His lap."

It seems that sometimes the veil is not immediately drawn at birth. A mother told of her little two-year-old sitting in on a conversation she was having with friends. They were discussing names and how we know the Lord's name and Heavenly Father's name but we don't know our Mother in Heaven's name. The little boy thought for a moment, then informed them, "Oh, her name is _____." [withheld] "Out of the mouths of babes . . ."

We have a little grandson who is full of life and fun, and sure of how much he is loved and how special he is. One day he came visiting with his parents. Grandma and Grandpa were upstairs where he couldn't see us immediately. But he ran into the house, threw down his coat, and called as loud as he could with his three-and-a-half-year-old voice, "I'm here!" We loved it. Those two words told a whole story.

Often we could be guided by the Spirit if we would be but very still and listen. We could know how special, how valuable, our children are to God.

One young mother had the following experience when just she and her baby were at home alone. The house was free of the noise of the TV, the radio, the telephone, and the older children's interruptions. As the mother was feeding her seven-month-old child, a beautiful and very strong thought impressed itself on her mind: "This sweet little girl, your daughter here, was very, very close and dearly loved by Mother in Heaven." This impression helped the mother keep her patience and softness when this same little girl had frequent tantrums in her early years.

One young man, returning home from church one Sunday afternoon after being ordained a teacher, walked into his room and felt a presence there. It gave him good, peaceful feelings, and he felt the presence was his deceased great-grandparents showing their happiness about the path he was choosing. Not knowing what to do or say in this situation, he just said, "Hi Grandma and Grandpa. I love you." Then he went to find his parents as usual.

It may well be that our young sons and daughters will become the fathers and mothers, the grandfathers and grandmothers, of those spirits who have been withheld to come forth at this time and be the leaders when Jesus Christ comes to the earth again. What an awesome responsibility! What a noble calling! Our youth need to know this and they also need to be taught to live appropriately.

Teach children to be "temple worthy" from childhood on. They are capable of learning much at a very young age. Reinforce good behavior. Kindly change undesirable behavior—as quickly as possible.

We can often "stand all amazed" at the good acts and the thoughts and words our children seem to have—an intuitive inheritance. As we as parents strive diligently to teach them, often they in pure innocence teach us.

Elder Neal A. Maxwell has observed: "Inspired children often show the way through the wilderness. . . . Children often have the 'thoughts and [the] intents of [their] hearts' focused on the Master (Mosiah 5:13). Though not full of years, such children are full of faith! Too young for formal Church callings, they have been 'called to serve' as exemplifiers, doing especially well when blessed with 'goodly parents' (1 Nephi 1:1)."[12]

At times we may innocently let a child's undesirable behavior continue without realizing that it will be a real detriment to the child later. Be careful of permissiveness. It can be part of the problem. "Permissiveness does not show love—nor can you buy a child's love."[13]

We can become so desensitized by the evils of today's world that we begin to accept wrong actions. A few simple anchors early on give strength to withstand evil forces. As we read Joshua 24:15, it instructs us, "Choose you this day whom ye will serve . . . but as for me and my house, we will serve the Lord."

There is an old saying my grandmother used: "A stitch in time saves nine." That philosophy can be right for many instances in life. For instance, we may not worry too much about a child trying a cigarette, but the Surgeon General's Report of 1995 advises: "Nearly all first use of tobacco occurs before high school graduation; this finding suggests that if adolescents can be kept tobacco-free, most will never start using tobacco. . . . Tobacco is often the first drug used by those young people who use alcohol, marijuana, and other drugs."[14]

On April 30, 1998, the National Foundation to End Teen Pregnancy put out the results of a recent survey taken from conferring with hundreds of teens. "Parental guidance is more important than birth control means in preventing teen pregnancy. This is especially true when parents convey their values and principles to their children."[15]

President J. Reuben Clark Jr. emphasized: "I appeal to you parents, take nothing for granted about your children. The great bulk of them, of course, are good, but some of us do not know when they begin to go away from the path of truth and righteousness. Be watchful every day and hour. Never relax your care, your solicitude. Rule kindly in the spirit of the gospel and the spirit of the priesthood, but rule, if you wish your children to follow the right path."[16]

In the April 1929 general conference Elder Orson F. Whitney quoted the Prophet Joseph Smith on the matter of wayward children: "The eye of the Shepherd is upon them. . . . Pray for your careless and disobedient children; hold onto them with your faith. Hope on, trust on till you see the salvation of God."[17]

President Ezra Taft Benson, in his inspiring sermon to the children of the Church given in the April 1989 general conference, gave many guidelines for children to follow and for parents to guide their children:

1. Prayer—every day. Ask for help and give thanks.
2. Honor your fathers and mothers.
3. Enjoy and respect your grandparents.
4. Be a real friend to your brothers and sisters.
5. Choose friends who have high ideals—who help you to be good.
6. Attend sacrament meeting. Listen carefully.
7. Enjoy Primary and attend every week. Bring your nonmember friends. Learn the songs. Memorize the Articles of Faith. Earn the Gospel in Action Award.
8. Be honest. Do not lie. Do not steal. Do not cheat.
9. Be clean in your thought and speech.
10. Be a true Latter-day Saint. Dare to do right.
11. Avoid books, magazines, videos, movies, and television shows that are not good.
12. Avoid the very appearance of evil.
13. Stay away from: pornography, drugs, profanity, and immorality.
14. Dress modestly.
15. Be courteous and polite.
16. Live the Word of Wisdom.
17. Keep the Sabbath day holy.
18. Listen to good music.

19. Be a good student.
20. Begin your own library of favorite tapes, books, and pictures.
21. Read each month *The Friend* and *New Era* magazines.
22. Be a good citizen. Be patriotic. Love your country.
23. Prepare for a mission [this for able young men].
24. Learn homemaking skills.
25. If you do not feel safe or are frightened, please talk to someone who can help you—a parent, a teacher, your bishop, or a friend.

Referring again to the Nephite children who were visited by angels, President Benson said: "I promise you, dear children, that angels will minister unto you also. You may not see them, but they will be there to help you, and you will feel of their presence."[18]

Dear parents, mothers, fathers, we must behold our children as soon as they are born, then continue to behold them, teach them, love them, pray for them and with them as they grow, so that one day we can behold them back with Heavenly Father, surrounded by angelic beings in an eternal home, hopefully with all of us there also.

NOTES

1. Henry B. Eyring, "To Draw Closer to God," *Ensign,* May 1991, pp. 66, 67.

2. M. R. Lybbert, "The Special Status of Children," *Ensign,* May 1994, p. 31.

3. Brenda Hunter, "Who's Minding the Children?" *Focus on the Family,* May 1998, p. 11.

4. From author's personal notes.

5. H. Burke Peterson, "Mother, Catch the Vision of Your Call," *Ensign,* May 1974, pp. 31, 32.

6. Virginia U. Jensen, "Creating Places of Security," *Ensign,* November 1997, p. 90.

7. Zig Ziglar, *Raising Positive Kids in a Negative World* [New York: Ballantine Books, 1985], pp. 117–18.

8. Pablo Casals, *The Secrets of Strong Families* [New York: Berkley Books, 1985], p. 47.

9. First Presidency, *Improvement Era,* April 27, 1915, p. 734.

10. Marion G. Romney, "The Book of Mormon," *Ensign,* May 1980, p. 67.

11. Sister Carol Ann Nawracaj, *Treasures from Heaven* (New York: Penguin Group, 1997), p. 1.

12. Neal A. Maxwell, " 'Becometh As a Child,' " *Ensign*, May 1996, p. 69.

13. Delbert L. Stapley, "The Value of Love," *Improvement Era*, December 1970, p. 65.

14. "Preventing Tobacco Use Among Young People," *Surgeon General's Report*, 1995, p. 5.

15. From author's personal notes.

16. J. Reuben Clark Jr., *Improvement Era*, May 1948, p. 312.

17. Orson F. Whitney, in Conference Report, April 1929, p. 110.

18. Ezra Taft Benson, "To the Children of the Church," *Ensign*, May 1989, p. 83.

CHAPTER THREE

The Covenant to Love and Bear Witness ✓

"And behold, ye are the children of the prophets;
and ye are of the House of Israel; and ye are of the
covenant which the Father made with your fathers,
saying unto Abraham: And in thy seed shall all
the kindreds of the earth be blessed. The Father
having raised me up unto you first, and sent me to
bless you in turning away every one of you from
his iniquities; and this because ye are children of
the covenant."
—3 NEPHI 20:25–26

by
Angie T. Hinckley

*It took me a minute to realize that my preschoolers were having a religious discussion with their young neighbor. . . .
I walked past the room a time or two and caught part of a
three-degrees-of-glory discussion.*

"I desperately want my children to see at least something in their earthly father that would encourage their belief in a dependable, compassionate, and loving God."

JEFFREY R. HOLLAND

*A*s a young child, life seemed simple. I had a loving family, and I knew that I was a child of God, just as I often sang in Primary. At age eight I was baptized and confirmed, which felt like the right thing to do. But as a teenager, my life became more complicated. My patriarchal blessing revealed that along with being a child of God and of my earthly parents, I was also a descendent of Abraham, through the house of Israel. At the time this was a mystery. I wondered not only "Lord, how is it done?" but more significantly, "Why is it necessary?" Although I knew that Abraham was a great prophet who made a covenant with the Lord, as a young person I understood neither the importance nor the responsibility of my being among Abraham's descendants.

Now, many years later, as a parent of my own four teenagers I am beginning to understand both the honor and the burden of this heritage. I now realize that when my father baptized and confirmed me, I established not only my membership in Christ's church but also my membership in the family of Abraham as one of the "children of the covenant." As the Apostle Paul said, "For as many of you as have been baptized into Christ have put on Christ. . . . And if ye be Christ's, then are ye Abraham's seed, and heirs according to the promise" (Galatians 3:27, 29).

But my baptism was only the first of many actions that would affirm my covenant relationship with the Lord. Weekly I renew my baptismal covenant through the sacrament and try to keep the Sabbath day as a "perpetual covenant" (Exodus 31:16). I have also received the Lord's endowment and been married in his temple. After

---

Angie T. Hinckley and her husband, Stuart, are the parents of two sons and two daughters. She has served in many Church assignments, including as a counselor in a stake Relief Society presidency and as ward Young Women president. She holds a bachelor's degree in English and has written a booklet about Church presidents for the Relief Society Beneral Board.

many years I have come to understand that in every dispensation "the gospel (including the priesthood and all the necessary ordinances) is bestowed by God upon man, and received by covenant."[1] The full blessings of the gospel are made available to us only as we strive to comprehend them, and desire them, and are ready to receive them by covenant.

The blessings promised to the house of Israel are truly magnificent, including the rights to the priesthood and all the "blessings of the Gospel, which are the blessings of salvation, even of life eternal." Along with these blessings is the responsibility to teach and "bear this ministry and Priesthood unto all nations" (Abraham 2:9, 11).

The Lord specifically chose to bestow His blessings on Abraham because of Abraham's faithfulness and his dedication to teaching his posterity the gospel. The Lord said, "For I know him, that he will command his children and his household after him, and they shall keep the way of the Lord, to do justice and judgment" (Genesis 18:19). Each generation must prepare the next to understand and live these covenants. It is a responsibility inherited by all who are children of the covenant. As Elder Henry B. Eyring has stated: "The power of that covenant to love and to witness should transform what members do . . . in the family. . . . For a person not yet a member of the Church, to fail to provide such moments of love and faith is simply a lost opportunity. But for those under covenant, it is much more. There are few places where the covenant to love and to bear witness is more easily kept than in the home. And there are few places where it can matter more for those for whom we are accountable."[2]

As we focus on this responsibility I think we will realize that there are many ways we are now building or have already built a strong foundation for our children to make these commitments. And with further reflection we will be able to think of many more things, often seemingly small things, we can still do that will continue to prepare them. I am reminded of a phrase from the Young Women theme that young Latter-day Saint women repeat each Sunday in their opening exercises, "as we come to accept and act upon these values we will be prepared to make and keep sacred covenants." The Young Women values being referred to are also repeated weekly: faith, divine nature, individual worth, knowledge, choice and accountability, good works, and integrity. When I compared these values to my thoughts about what is needed as a foundation for making and keeping covenants, I was struck by how similar they were. I am grateful for the programs of the Church already in place to help us teach our children these important truths.

As parents we have the privilege to help form our children's concept of the nature of God. If our children can come to see God as a loving, unchanging, and all-knowing Father, they can learn to have faith that He will keep His promises. They will believe that the Lord "doeth not anything save it be for the benefit of the world; for he loveth the world" (2 Nephi 26:24). The stories of Abraham, Noah, Ruth, Nephi, Enos, and Alma are only a few of the many from the scriptures that will help us teach our children that we can trust the promises of the Lord. "I, the Lord, am bound when ye do what I say" (D&C 82:10) is a truth that can be experienced even by a child. Personal and family prayer is another way in which even a very young child can become acquainted with a loving and all-knowing Father. We can also testify of the Lord's goodness in our lives by gratefully and frequently acknowledging to our children the blessings we have received.

Still another way in which our children learn of the nature of their Heavenly Father is from their interactions with us, their earthly parents. Though we are subject to many human failings, our effort to be patient, long-suffering, and trustworthy will be stored in the memory of our children and used as a reference for understanding such qualities in their heavenly parents. Elder Jeffrey R. Holland stated, "I desperately want my children to see at least something in their earthly father that would encourage their belief in a dependable, compassionate, and loving God."[3] Even our feeble efforts to teach and emulate the divine nature of God will be magnified in the lives of our children, and their faith and trust in God will increase along with a desire to share their understanding.

While he was in law school my husband's time during the week was mostly taken up with classes and studying, but he made an effort to read with our two preschoolers, Caroline and Rob, right after dinner before returning to his studies. They all "read" together from their own set of illustrated scripture stories of the standard works of the

Church. The children enjoyed this time with their father, and they quickly made it through all the books, but I didn't realize the impact it was having until almost a year later.

We were living in Las Vegas across the street from a wonderful Catholic family who had a young daughter close to the ages of our own children. One day while they were playing together in our home, our son Rob came running into the kitchen anxiously saying, "Mom, where are the books, Victoria doesn't believe." It took me a minute to realize that my preschoolers were having a religious discussion with their young neighbor. Rob was obviously concerned over his friend's lack of understanding, but seemed sure that his "scriptures" would set her straight. Armed with the Book of Mormon, the Doctrine and Covenants, and Bible scripture stories he went back to the playroom. I walked past the room a time or two and caught part of a three-degrees-of-glory discussion.

Victoria left soon afterwards. I asked my children how it had gone, and Rob expressed his concern that she still did not believe. We speculated that her lack of faith might be due to her not knowing all the scriptures. Caroline immediately asked if we should let her borrow ours.

I realized from this experience of watching my children's spontaneous "bearing of testimony" to their friend that the responsibility of the covenant "to bear this ministry" will flow naturally from a desire to share our understanding of a loving Father. Fortified with a firm faith in a loving and all-knowing Heavenly Father, our children will be prepared to faithfully endure and confidently trust, even when faced with difficult times.

One difficult time for my children that did come not many years later was the early death of one of their cousins. It affected all of us—each of the children in an individual way—but he was in age just a year older than Caroline, making the loss especially poignant for her. She wrote in her journal: "I always looked up to him. He had been the first to do so many things and set a good example for the rest of us to follow." Believing that God is loving and wise helped her to trust that "all things shall work together for your good" (D&C 90:24) and to find peace in knowing that all His promises will be fulfilled if we do our part.

One "good" that has benefitted all the cousins, and others who knew Sean, is related to the covenant. In spite of having lived only seventeen years, and despite illness that had stripped him of all but the barest modicum of strength, he seemed to understand what it meant to bear the priesthood of God. And if he could not bear it to all the world, he would bear it to all he knew with all the power he had. In this he left a legacy of devotion to duty and the covenant responsibility to the priesthood that has been and will continue to be an inspiration to those who knew him.

A close friend speaking at the funeral related an experience shortly before Sean's death: "After Sunday School I noticed Sean in the foyer, waiting for priesthood meeting to begin. His tired, feeble physical body was braced up against a wall . . . because he didn't have the strength to stand. . . . I offered to take him home for some much-needed rest, but he said he needed to go to priesthood meeting . . . After opening exercises, I again pleaded . . . In a weak, soft voice, he again responded that he needed to attend priesthood meeting." With friends helping they were able to get him up the steep stairs to his classroom. "In [seeing Sean's effort] that five minutes I learned more about courage and determination than I had in the previous forty-eight years of my life. . . . It occurred to me why this was so important to Sean. This would be the last priesthood meeting he would attend in his mortal life. After class he was helped down, then he rested until he had strength enough to go to the car. . . . Sean loved the Lord, and he loved holding the Aaronic Priesthood. . . . Many times I had wondered what it really means to magnify one's priesthood. . . . I have no longer reason to wonder."[4]

Although, as King Benjamin points out, we are always in God's debt, His blessings now and in the future far outweigh our contributions (see Mosiah 2:20–24); a covenant always implies a two-sided agreement. When we remember that without the Atonement, promised from beginning, all our efforts would be to no avail, our obedience to His commandments seems a small part that is required from us. And yet our children may come to trust that their Heavenly Father will do whatever He has promised, but they may still lack confidence in their own ability to do what is their part. After introducing Himself to Moses as the "Lord God Almighty . . . Endless is my name" the Lord taught Moses something about his own nature: "And behold thou art my son . . . and thou art in the similitude of mine Only Begotten" (Moses 1:4, 6). Likewise we need to teach children not only faith in Heavenly Father but also to recognize and believe in their own potential as His children. How we view the commandments of our Heavenly Father will ultimately influence our belief in ourselves. If our children are taught that Heavenly Father will never require us to do what we are not capable of learning or becoming, they will come to see the commandments, which are essentially our part of keeping the covenants, as a guide to or description of their potential. This will be reinforced by the prompting thoughts and feelings concerning the laws Heavenly Father gives us as a sign of His covenant. In renewing His covenant with the house of Israel, the Lord states:

"For this is the covenant that I will make with the house of Israel after those days, saith the Lord; I will put my laws into their mind, and write them in their hearts: and I will be to them a God, and they shall be to me a people: . . . for all shall know me, from the least to the greatest" (Hebrews 8:10–11).

If we as parents encourage our children to see His commandments as personal goals that they will be motivated to keep by feelings and thoughts from our Heavenly Father, they will feel the confidence to reach toward their potential as His children.

Preparing children to keep covenants includes teaching them how to keep their hearts and minds open to the influence of the Spirit. We can help a child recognize the prompting of the Holy Ghost and be sensitive to things that might make them more or less receptive to this direction. I remember that as a young mother I received from my visiting teacher a message on the Holy Ghost. In doing so she shared with me some advice she had received from her mother-in-law on how to recognize when you are being prompted by the Holy Ghost. Her advice was simply: If you feel directed to do something good, do it, and by acting upon that feeling you will become more aware of how and when you are influenced.

I liked this advice because it reminded me of a scripture in the Doctrine and Covenants that was important to me as a teenager, when I was afraid of doing lots of things that might lead to my embarrassment, including such minor things as saying hello to people I didn't know very well or offering help to someone who had just dropped her books in the hall. Somehow I found courage to follow such promptings from Doctrine and Covenants 6:34, 36: "Fear not, little flock; do good; . . . Look unto me in every thought; doubt not, fear not."

Along with the confidence "to do good," a child must also be given the opportunities to increase his own abilities through experience. It may seem obvious that a child needs to be encouraged to do what he can to make a contribution, but it is surprising how often parents do for a child what he can do or could learn to do for himself. Perhaps they think that such helpfulness is a display of affection, or they simply lack the time and patience that it takes to let a child do it. "Here, just let me do it," is a common demand from the hurried parents of small children.

Fostering helplessness deprives a child of the satisfaction of learning competence and of being useful. Although the child's contribution to his own needs and the needs of the family will of necessity be very small and at first full of mishaps, a child learns to trust himself as he is allowed to try, and learns to put forth an effort when it is met with appreciation. As parents we can learn from how our Heavenly Father deals with His children. Always some effort is required, even if it is only the desire to believe, to ask, to knock, or to ponder. Our Heavenly Father allows us to be needed, even to be necessary, in helping Him bless others' lives as well as our own.

Our relationship in a family is one of interdependence and it requires much thought and wisdom to know what participation will allow a child to grow and feel needed without overburdening him. Children can sense when they are making a positive difference and will soon come to understand that they can "do many things of their own free will, and bring to pass much righteousness" (D&C 58:27).

Encouraging participation can lead to instilling persistence. As we respond with patience to initial failures and with support to additional attempts, we give our children the hope they need to keep trying.

When our son Bryant was three he started swimming lessons at a neighborhood pool. He approached the water with trepidation that soon turned to fear. After a few minutes in the water he was climbing out and begging to go home. I tried to comfort and encourage him by whispering, "Come on, you can do it, you don't want to be a quitter." He stopped shivering and crying long enough to yell loudly, "I am a quitter."

Obviously mine was not the right approach, nor an option I wanted him to have. With some additional coaxing we had him tentatively back in the pool, and at the end of the lesson his teacher casually and cheerfully said, "We'll see you tomorrow, Bryant." His response was a mumbled, "My mom will be talking to you." As you can imagine he got most of the talking to and was back in the pool the next day. Bryant is now an accomplished swimmer with several years on a swim team to contradict his earlier statement.

Persistence is also a necessary prerequisite quality for repentance. Avoiding discouragement and even disillusionment will be more important to our eventual success in life than our beginning enthusiasm or skill.

Our children will find it easier to keep the promises they make if they have been taught to be dependable. Our taking advantage of seemingly minor occasions that teach dependability helps prepare a child to accept more responsibility with integrity. Since Christie, at fifteen, has learned to be reliable in calling home by a specific time as requested when she is out with her friends on the weekend, she will be better prepared to accept the accountability of being an employee at sixteen or seventeen. This lesson becomes increasingly valuable as young persons learn to face fearlessly the discomfort of meeting obligations rather than the disrespect they show others and earn themselves by being unreliable.

Each of our four children has taken music lessons and has found occasion to ask me to cancel a lesson at the last minute that they were not ready for or that conflicted with a better option that had come up. Although there have been a few times when lessons had to be canceled due to sickness or hazardous weather conditions, usually these requests were just another opportunity to teach the need to be dependable. Their teachers were counting on them, time had been reserved, and we had agreed to pay for that time; all of this was more important than avoiding some discomfort or putting off some pleasure. Invariably learning to be dependable involves learning to sacrifice some immediate convenience or comfort. A child who learns that he can do what is needed to be dependable will have the courage and faith in himself to make lasting commitments.

Choosing to make such commitment requires loving effort. As a young child I also took music lessons, and I remember clearly thinking how wise I was to finally come up with a reason why I should quit. I recall telling my mother that I would be willing to trade learning to play the piano for a happy childhood. Not practicing seemed to me to ensure the happy childhood, and I thought that would be sufficient payback for not being able to play the piano for the rest of my life. Such a shallow perspective may be typical of a young person but it illustrates the necessity of teaching children to make choices that lead to their own or someone else's growth and may not be immediately gratifying or easy.

We can help a child ask, "What can I learn from doing this?" or "What can I share by participating in this activity that might help someone else?" not just "Will it be fun?" or "Will there be food?" when faced with the inevitable choices of what activities to be involved in. This life is designed to challenge us and give us opportunities for growth and service. By encouraging such choices we can help our children learn that consistent effort is rewarded with accomplishment and that giving service brings a feeling of wholeness that can be found in no other way. Through experience they will come to see service and growth as a precious part of their birthright as "children of the covenant."

The more understanding we as parents have about what it means to be "children of the covenant," the better able we will be to use everyday opportunities, often seemingly insignificant ones, to build the foundation our children need to keep the covenants they will be making. Elder Eyring has cautioned: "To neglect those opportunities is a choice not to keep sacred covenants. Because God always honors covenants, I can make a promise to those who in faith keep the covenant to create experiences of giving love and bearing testimony with their families. They will reap a harvest of hearts touched, faith in Jesus Christ exercised unto repentance, and the desire and the power to keep covenants strengthened."[5]

Each small step prepares our children for a next, bigger step. My hope is that "bearing this ministry" by serving a full-time mission will seem as necessary and doable for my sons as sharing their understanding of the gospel with a playmate or persevering through swimming lessons was at age three. It is my hope too that as they grow in knowledge and skills, each of our four children will feel prepared to accept the responsibilities of the covenant to teach their own families and to serve faithfully in the Church, knowing that they can "go and do [what] the Lord hath commanded, for [they] know that the Lord giveth no commandments unto the children of men, save he shall prepare a way for them that they may accomplish the thing which he commandeth them" (1 Nephi 3:7).

As we diligently follow the example of our father Abraham and teach our children to keep the ways of the Lord, they will come to understand the great blessings of their heritage as "children of the prophets" and learn that to be God's people is to know of His love and share that message with the world. "Know therefore that the Lord thy God, he is God, the faithful God, which keepeth covenant and mercy with them that love him and keep his commandments to a thousand generations" (Deuteronomy 7:9).

NOTES

1. George S. Tate, "Covenants in Biblical Times," *Encyclopedia of Mormonism,* vol. 1 (New York: Macmillan Publishing Co., 1992), pp. 333–34.

2. Henry B. Eyring, "Witnesses for God," *Ensign,* November 1996, pp. 31–32.

3. Jeffrey R. Holland and Patricia T. Holland, "Considering Covenants: Women, Men, Perspective, Promises," in *To Rejoice as Women,* ed. Susette Fletcher Green and Dawn Hall Anderson (Salt Lake City: Deseret Book Co., 1995), p. 114.

4. Taken from a talk given at Sean's funeral by Ron Beach. A transcript of the funeral is in the author's personal files.

5. Eyring, p. 32.

CHAPTER FOUR

Come unto Him, to Joy and Peace

"O thou afflicted, tossed with tempest, and not
comforted! Behold, I will lay thy stones with fair
colors, and lay thy foundations with sapphires. And
I will make thy windows of agates, and thy gates of
carbuncles, and all thy borders of pleasant stones.
And all thy children shall be taught of the Lord;
and great shall be the peace of thy children."
—ISAIAH 54:11–13; 3 NEPHI 22:11–13

by
Francine R. Bennion

*If we look with compassion on our own young ones and lead
them toward peace, wherever we are with them can become a
fruitful haven, a watered garden, whatever their current hard
ground, weeds, and drought.*

"These things I have spoken unto you, that in me ye might have peace. In
the world ye shall have tribulation: but be of good cheer; I have overcome
the world."

JOHN 16:33

*O*UR GOD KNOWS US. GOD LOOKS WITH compassion on us and
our hopes and fatigues, and in a thousand ways invites us to come to
Him, to joy and peace. Jesus, Isaiah, and others affirm this not only
as a matter of hope or faith but also as absolute reality. I too affirm
this as absolute undeniable reality, for I have experience of it.

If we look with compassion on our own young ones and lead
them toward peace, wherever we are with them can become a fruitful haven, a watered garden, whatever their current hard ground,
weeds, and drought.

We thank God for His good promises of peace and give peace
many meanings. Peace is victory over enemies, freedom from enemies, or having no enemies; peace is relief from pain; peace is finding answers; peace is justice; peace is having everyone do what you
want them to do, and nothing else; peace is the comfortable companionship of good family, friends, and God.

But if our children believe peace exists only where there is no
war, pain, disagreement, confusion, injustice, or loneliness, they will
not taste peace in this world where lions do eat lambs and asps bite.

Hated, mocked, stoned, ignored, misunderstood, betrayed, expecting thorns, Gethsemane, and crucifixion, Jesus spoke of present
peace, not only peace in a distant time and place: "Peace I leave with
you, my peace I give unto you: not as the world giveth, give I unto
you. Let not your heart be troubled, neither let it be afraid" (John
14:27).

Jesus did not promise that as we become more like Him our exis-

---

*FRANCINE R. BENNION and her husband, Robert, live in Provo, Utah, and are the
parents of three children. Francine holds degrees from Brigham Young University
and Ohio State, and has taught at both of these universities. She has served on the
General Church Writing Committee and the General Boards of Young Women and
Relief Society.*

tence will become smoothly uneventful. Jesus did not offer peace only when all sinners have perished, the world is a perfect sea of glass, and a celestial kingdom becomes home. He told His disciples: "These things I have spoken unto you, that in me ye might have peace. In the world ye shall have tribulation: but be of good cheer; I have overcome the world" (John 16:33). Acquainted body and soul with grief, Jesus offered peace in this world as it is now, and also in more glorious times to come.

If our young ones are to know the peace that passes common understanding, the great peace promised us and our children, they must know what that precious peace is not. Peace cannot be the absence of struggle, confusion, or agony, for these can exist as long as unfettered agents exist. Peace is not a Utopian earth, or a traditionally-conceived heaven where we sit on soft seats in sweet serenity strumming soothing zithers, or an isolated schoolroom where all obedient souls miraculously absorb godhood. Our God, if we are to believe our whole body of scriptures and the history of our world, does not sit in such a heaven.

If we are to have peace now in our inexperience and relative ignorance, or later as we and our young ones become more like Elohim and Jehovah, the peace must be in ourselves. If eternal peace requires that God prevent all fear, we will spend eternity fearing fear. If peace requires that God preserve one person by keeping others from exercising their agency, we will live not in peace but in tyranny.

Those of us who hope to become more like our Father and Jesus did not come to earth only so that we might escape it and return to God unchanged; nor did Jesus Himself. Contemplating the bitter cup He would drink, and was drinking, Jesus said, "Now is my soul troubled; and what shall I say? Father, save me from this hour: but for this cause came I unto this hour" (John 12:27).

We came to meet things as they are and have been, that we might become more than we have yet been and begin to be with God and Jesus more richly. Whatever we encounter with other humans, our physical universe, and our own selves is part of that process. In trouble struggle, soaring triumph, or ordinary daily tasks, we are preparing to meet God and Jesus face to face with greater capacities than we now have.

Children may not believe what we tell them of peace if their experience with us contradicts what we say. One of the great gifts adults can give young ones is affirmation of peace as a reality, not with words alone but with experiences. Though we cannot bequeath inescapable inner peace to our children, and may be in the process of struggling to create it for ourselves, we can create tools of peace and model ways by which they may begin to create their own peace in a complex world.

Every teaching of Jesus, every public law, countless books, and many conferences are intended to promote peace. Here are a few relevant considerations regarding our world, our selves, our communities, and our God.

Personal peace is difficult for persons constantly surprised that things are not as they had hoped. It is important not only to hope for the ideal but also to study and meet present realities. Help young persons to understand that because God preserves human agency and a lawful physical universe, humans do experience injustice, hunger, and catastrophe as well as a great diversity of good persons, places, objects, and events to enjoy, and a variety of ways to understand and address any issue. Discuss with them events and people in your community, your country, and around the world, asking questions, evaluating effective ways to address issues, and looking at what contributions you and your children might make together or separately, now or in the future.

We can hardly know inner peace if we do not begin to comprehend war. We can hardly appreciate a country's peace if we know nothing of the struggles that preceded it. Our scriptures urge us to seek to understand our world by experience and by learning of things both in heaven and in the earth as set forth in the best books. (See, for example, sections 88 and 93 in the Doctrine and Covenants.)

It has been said we should not bother reading or listening to news reports because they are not accurate and reliable. Sometimes, however, they are the only clues we have to what is happening beyond our own street. We can learn to make good use of imperfect clues and tools, for example, by asking each other follow-up questions in ordinary conversations rather than making snap judgments, not bothering with details, and never considering any viewpoint except our own.

(On the other hand, at times one must acknowledge the impossibility of knowing or understanding, and must do what seems best. When our children were on the verge of no longer needing baby-sitters I offered to give them the money I would give a baby-sitter, but only if they did not fight. The first time we came home they met us with lively reports of who had started arguments and who had suffered injustice—which we took as evidence that they did fight. We had no way of assigning fault: we simply offered to get a baby-sitter next time, which proved unnecessary.)

One mother said we do not need to read newspapers or understand world events because all we have to worry about is our own righteousness and that of our children. Our young people live in the world, however, not only in their parents' arms. Jesus suggested that our love should extend beyond ourselves and our own, which is difficult for young ones who remain ignorant, vulnerable, and helpless. Let us help our children begin to address problems within their capacities at any age and not just wish problems didn't exist or expect a parent (resentful or "noble") to take care of all problems for them. Let us help them to meet things as they are, not yearn for a different world that does not exist or ignore all lives but their own.

Peace in this world lies not in doing away with all trouble but in being secure in the midst of it. Such security is what old folktales and myths commonly told to children have been about: persons' courage, wit, kindness, or resourcefulness, combined with supernatural aid, help them become invulnerable to grave dangers and ultimately alive and successful in their quests.

We have some similar stories in our scriptures where God's assistance enhances the power of the righteous; for example, Joseph's resourcefulness in Egypt and David's courage against Goliath. When the sons of Mosiah want to go among their enemies, the Lamanites, Mosiah asks God if this is a good idea, and God replies, "Let them go up . . . and I will deliver thy sons out of the hands of the Lamanites" (Mosiah 28:7). Like so many before me, I too yearned for such a promise when I first read of it: I would go confidently through anything if I had the promise that I would eventually survive safe and well.

We all have that promise. We and our young ones can survive anything and transcend everything, though sometimes only after resurrection. Though our Father does not prevent or erase all that may disturb us, He invites us to become more courageous, kind, and resourceful and makes us invulnerable to ultimate loss of our selves, if that is what we want. Jesus teaches us to attain peace and freedom and to exercise our capacity to change as we meet enemies or neighbors, lilies or camels, and He shows us that even though we die we will live.

My grandchildren love hero stories and ask me to make them up day and night when I'm with them. When I was young I myself loved stories about sons or daughters who transcended dragons, mountains, witches, wizards, oceans, mountains, grey women, dogs with eyes as big as dinner plates, dancing shoes, wolves, or whatever threatened. I felt myself a hero in such tales, but I discovered my own vulnerability and fear, as well as delight and joy, in real life.

It is good to begin playing heroic virtues in imagination, but it is essential to invent and discover them for oneself in reality. Children who discover their own capacities to work, be courageous, make sacrifices, and endure pain, and who trust themselves under stress, become more fit to find peace in our complex world. When I began hiking with one of my sons and his family up the steep mountainside to Timpanogas Cave, the grandchild walking with me became terrified of the height and begged to go back down, which at that point would have been just as difficult as to continue up. Scarcely daring to move his feet, his teeth chattering, he clung to rocks lining the inside of the trail. I stayed with him, assuring him he could do it, making clear there was nothing to do but keep going, sometimes talking about what he was experiencing and sometimes distracting him with other questions and talk, unobtrusively staying between him and the edge of the wide paved trail where it dropped off to steep slopes, praising him for his courage, and showing him a little brown lizard.

Near the top he said resignedly, "I just want to go back, but that doesn't seem to make any difference." It is true. Sometimes you have to keep going, as I discovered years ago on a high snowbound trail across steeper slopes on that same mountain, and as Jesus knew when contemplating the cup He would drink, first asking, "If it be possible, let this cup pass from me," but then praying a second time, "If this cup may not pass away from me, except I drink it . . ." (Matthew 26:39, 42).

My grandson reached the cave, liked the stalactites, the stalagmites, and other wondrous formations, asked the guide good questions, came back out into the sunlight, and literally skipped the whole mile and a half down the steep trail to the car. Sometimes a child needs to be protected, cared for, rescued, cradled, or soothed, but there are also growing times when they need to be allowed to discover their capacities. We can give them both kinds of help, not only one or the other, to help them overcome fear of fear.

Some years ago on National Public Radio I heard a Bosnian woman say, as her home was being shelled, "They haven't won yet; they haven't made us hate them"; and more recently, in the middle of his country's economic and political breakdown, I heard a Russian man say, "We've been scared so many times that as long as we have head and hands we'll survive." Understanding of God's ways and trust in one's own capacities are powerful realities.

A healthy child of normal capacities who is repeatedly threatened by adults with punishment may become fearful or rebellious rather than peaceful. A child who is constantly offered rewards may become greedy, self-centered, or dissatisfied, particularly in the larger world where apparent rewards are more scarce. The inherent rewards of what is good, like the inherent sorrows of what is not, are less likely to become apparent to children who always see external incentives attached to everything an adult wants them to do. Though there are times when punishment or reward may be useful because they are all a child can currently understand, most children grow to understand the manipulation inherent in them. Inner peace grows from understanding things as they are, and have been, and will be, not simply from trying to please a currently powerful person. Traditional Christianity has interpreted God as such a punisher-rewarder that it is difficult for many to recognize the great goodness of our Helper and the invitation to become more like Him because His are the ways of joy, freedom, and peace.

Peace can grow in gifts unexpected and unearned. Though some men have understood Him differently, Jesus said our Father in

Heaven makes His sun rise on the evil and on the good, and sends rain on the just and on the unjust (see Matthew 5:43–45). One day when I was walking the hills alone, I came upon my six-year-old neighbor MacKenzie and her friend Erika. Though I'd never had a conversation with them before, I said hi. They showed me small rocks and wildflowers they had collected and I asked what they liked about the rocks. I told them that on the path beyond I had smelled a wonderful flower fragrance and could not see the source. We went our separate ways.

A couple of hours later my doorbell rang, and I found on my doorstep their rocks and flowers. "Surprise!" they shouted, the start of an affectionate friendship that has endured, but was not on any agenda. Another good day my doorbell rang and there were Tom and Louise with cymbals I'd wanted since third grade: the gift was not only the cymbals but also their knowing my heart. Another day, busy and difficult, Dorothy brought me baskets of blueberries, and again the gift was not only berries but affection, as have been Aileen's rolls, Ila's flowers, and Bob's fruits and flowers. These gifts were not earned, not regular, not expected, not given because someone was supposed to do a nice thing. Though elusive for many in excruciating distress, belief in the possibility of divine peace may be rooted in experience with past kindnesses, thoughtful, unexpected, or rare, and not earned with gold-star/black-mark hopes and fears.

If we give children experience with food they find delicious, music they find beautiful, grasses and trees they enjoy dancing with in the wind, they may begin to acquire a taste for inherent goodness. Children who experience lively, active bodies, minds, and hearts in goodness and peace are more likely to want them than if they are bored. Peace is often broken by boredom. Inner peace is not the end of lively joy, but what makes it possible.

There is no peace in repeated threatening, whacking, smacking, screaming, screeching, squawking, or abuse of any kind. But neither is there peace in boredom, helplessness, wishy-washy passivity, or sweetness masking bitterness. If some children have been damaged by hearing adults fighting or becoming the target of adult anger, others have been damaged by sweet smiles, silent pain, or simmering resentment. God shows no fondness for the illusion of peace where it does not exist: "They have healed also the hurt of the daughter of my people slightly," wrote Jeremiah, "saying, Peace, peace; when there is no peace" (Jeremiah 6:14).

Differences among people can cause inconvenience, loneliness, violence, abuse, and injustice. These must be addressed, not ignored or buried in a shallow grave. Citizens who have discovered international peace treaties to be a sham have lost faith in peace itself, as can children in a home where pretense prevents real peace.

Peace is hard-won by persons of any age who feel lonely not because there are no others around but because there are no others who hear them or know them. Give children the peace of being heard and known. Listen to them. Discover what they are thinking. Do not assume you already know, because they must be thinking what you think they think. Once learning to play a Bach fugue I sat at the piano managing for the first time to make all things work together towards a magnificent climax when my young son reached up to the keyboard to try to stop my fingers from moving. "Mommy?" "Just a minute, Brett. I'm just about finished." "Mommy?" "Wait a minute, please." "Mommy?" The climax ruined, I took my hands off the keyboard expecting some trivial little question, and said impatiently, "What is it?" "Mommy? Mommy, I love you."

It can be equally disturbing to a child to be either the center of everyone's attention or never the center of anyone's attention. However, to be heard by an adult, and known as truly as possible by an adult, is a taste of peace.

Jesus says the sum of the search for peace is this: love God, and love your neighbor and yourself. To learn what this means, to learn more richly who we are and who God is, to learn to live and love more as God does, is a magnificent and awesome process.

Peace grows from direct experience with God. We talk of God, preach of God, and read of God. We file and cross-reference what has been said and recorded of God and His Son Jesus. We pray to God in Jesus' name. Some peace may be found in what we choose to believe of Them, and in ritual attention to Them, but great peace, joy, and uncommon love are to be found in our experience with Them, not just in knowing what has been said of Them and what we have thought of Them.

The purpose of our teaching young ones about God and God's commandments is to lead them to know God directly for themselves. The purpose of teaching them to pray to God with thanksgiving and personal requests is to lead them to a relationship with God. If our prayers are always only a recital of what we are wanting and thinking, our children will not learn from us to focus also on God and listen to God, to be still and know God. Perhaps one reason why God knows us so much better than we individually know God is that often in our prayers God is doing all the listening. God speaks through prophets and scriptures but also directly to the heart and soul of one able to listen, and to rejoice with Him in prayer.

If in family prayers and blessings on the food we speak directly, as indeed many of our children do, to our Father who loves us, who gives us sun and stars and oranges and almonds, who is with us and listening to us, and if we consider ourselves with Him and not just calling to Him, our children will experience pools of peace in our days and nights.

Peace with God to come is beyond our words, for our words are made on earth about human experience on earth. So unlike common experience among troubled persons is God's great promised peace that Isaiah and other prophets speak of it in metaphors about rare, seemingly impossible wonders—roads of rare precious jewels under our walking feet, all the trees of the field clapping their hands though trees don't have hands and couldn't clap them if they did, lame legs leaping, weak knees strengthened, the barren woman bearing children and forgetting the shame of her youth and the reproach of her widowhood, the woman forsaken or refused finding herself valued and loved, the blind seeing, children safe with poisonous reptiles, lambs safe with lions, wine and milk without money and without price, children taught in great peace by the Lord Himself.

We all are God's children. Now we and our young ones together may seek joy, search for greater understanding, struggle to love imperfect humans, begin to know the taste of peace even in war and suffering, and discover the difference between what is good and what is not. When we meet God and Jesus face to face, and know Them more richly because we have tried Their ways with our present limited abilities, then peace, joy, love, and truth united and inseparable can become ours.

"O thou afflicted, tossed with tempest, and not comforted! Behold, I will lay thy stones with fair colors, and lay thy foundations with sapphires. And I will make thy windows of agates, and thy gates of carbuncles, and all thy borders of pleasant stones. And all thy children shall be taught of the Lord; and great shall be the peace of thy children" (3 Nephi 22:11–13).

CHAPTER FIVE

Approval in a Glance

"His countenance did smile upon them."
—3 NEPHI 19:25

by
Barbara W. Winder

I sensed that hands in motion hadn't always meant "love pats" to him. . . . The reassurance of a sincere smile caused him to separate himself from the crowd of children and come close for a big hug.

"The world grows increasingly noisy. . . . This trend to more noise, more excitement, more contention, less restraint, less dignity, less formality is not coincidental, nor innocent, nor harmless."

BOYD K. PACKER

W̶E WERE STILL MEETING AFTER SCHOOL for midweek Primary. I loved greeting the children as they arrived weary from their day of study. The children were chatting as they approached the meetinghouse. I recognized a little blond, first-grade boy as one who came only to Primary, but to no other Church meetings. I especially wanted him to feel welcome. As they skipped by me, I reached out, almost spontaneously from love, to give him a little pat and a cheerful, "Welcome to Primary." But he cowered as my hand went up. Instantly, I sensed that hands in motion hadn't always meant "love pats" to him.

"Jamie," I said softly. Not catching his eye until then, and smiling, I went on, "Welcome to Primary." The reassurance of a sincere smile caused him to separate himself from the crowd of children and come close for a big hug.

The Savior blessed me with an extra dose of love for this child, and it needed to be shared. The smile gave Jamie confidence, helped him feel accepted and loved. It also helped prepare the way for him to be taught about Heavenly Father, His Son Jesus Christ, the Holy Ghost, and the wonderful plan of happiness.

The smiling countenance of our Savior in 3 Nephi 19:25 seems to reflect His approval of all that had been accomplished with the Nephites during His brief stay with them. He taught them the gospel. Because of their desire and faith they were obedient and received the Holy Ghost. The Savior prayed to the Father for their unity, "That they may believe in me, that I may be in them as thou, Father, art in me, that we may be one" (3 Nephi 19:23). They were humble and prayerful. And, "Jesus blessed them as they did pray unto him; and

---

BARBARA W. WINDER, *born at the "depth of the Depression," has achieved much. She has been an assistant temple matron, the national president of Lambda Delta Sigma, and board member and General President of the Relief Society. She has served with her husband, Richard, as he presided over two missions. They are the parents of four children.*

his countenance did smile upon them, and the light of his countenance did shine upon them, and behold they were as white as the
countenance and . . . the garments of Jesus" (v. 25). We are told that
nothing upon the earth could be so white. The Savior then went a
little way off and prayed again to the Father, saying: "Father, I thank
thee that thou hast purified those whom I have chosen, because of
their faith, and I pray for them, and also for them who shall believe
on their words, that they may be purified in me, through faith on
their words, even as they are purified in me" (v. 28). After He had
spoken these words, He went back to the people and found that they
were still steadfastly praying, "and he did smile upon them again" (v.
30). Three times He smiled upon them. Receiving this obvious
approval from their Savior helped them know of His love, and it
encouraged them to continue in His ways, just as my smile helped
and encouraged my young Primary friend, Jamie.

Following the pattern the Savior set in this scriptural passage,
parents can better fulfill their heavy responsibility for nurturing and
training their children. In this account Jesus teaches the Nephites that
we must train our children in word and by example. Then He nur-
tures them by His approving countenance, which encourages a con-
tinuation of this righteousness. Likewise, if we as parents can praise
and approve our children's attempts at goodness we will strengthen
them in their abilities to do good and to be good.

To prepare our children that the Lord may smile upon them we
must practice Christlike attributes ourselves. Such attributes are
found in the teachings of Alma to the people of Gideon. "I would that
ye should be humble, . . . submissive, . . . gentle; easy to be entreated;
full of patience and long-suffering; . . . temperate in all things, . . .
diligent in keeping the commandments of God at all times; asking for
whatsoever things ye stand in need, both spiritual and temporal;
always returning thanks unto God for whatsoever things ye do
receive. And see that ye have faith, hope, and charity, and then ye will
always abound in good works" (Alma 7:23–24). These attributes will
help us have the proper spirit as we train and nurture our children.

The carnal world thwarts our attempts to follow the teaching
pattern Jesus set. Elder Boyd K. Packer cautions: "The world grows
increasingly noisy. Clothing and grooming and conduct are looser

and sloppier and more disheveled. Raucous music, with obscene lyrics blasted through amplifiers while lights flash psychedelic colors, characterizes the drug culture. Variations of these things are gaining wide acceptance and influence over our youth. . . . This trend to more noise, more excitement, more contention, less restraint, less dignity, less formality is not coincidental, nor innocent, nor harmless."[1]

President Gordon B. Hinckley also warned us that we cannot teach our precious young people if we lack Christlike attributes. He said, "The flower of love fades in an atmosphere of criticism and carping, of mean words and uncontrolled anger. Love flies out the window as contention enters."[2] A Chinese proverb teaches us, "If you are patient in one moment of anger, you will escape a hundred days of sorrow." Certainly we want to control our emotions, that our children can feel love and peace and that we might in harmony teach our children about the good things of life.

One thing social scientists have discovered is that often-praised children become more intelligent than often-blamed ones. There is a creative element in praise. Expressing appreciation and giving a sincere compliment for lessons well learned and lives well lived is another important quality Alma teaches, "My soul doth exceedingly rejoice, because of the exceeding diligence and heed which ye have given unto my word" (Alma 7:26). Positive reward for conscientious effort, like the Savior's smile upon the Nephites, is the comforting reassurance needed to reinforce good behavior.

Here is an example of an adult who through the thoughtful courtesies of a gracious heart built confidence and unlocked love in a small boy. Elizabeth Byrd, an American writer traveled to Inverness, Scotland, several years ago and recalled "a big rawboned farm woman sitting beside me on the bus [who] asked why an American should travel north in the dead of winter. It's rooky weather in the Highlands."

I explained that I liked wild weather and that I was gathering material for a historical novel, talking to country people, soaking up sheeplore and folkways that have changed little in four centuries.

[The Scottish woman] invited me to visit her overnight. "We've a wee croft, but warm, and I'd welcome your company, for my husband's off to market."

It was raining hard when we reached her home, a dumpy stone cottage on a bleak slope. Collies welcomed us and Mrs. McIntosh led me into a spotless, shabby parlor.

Suddenly the lights flickered and died. She sighed, "The power's oot," and lit candles. While she was making a fire there was a knock on the door.

She opened it and a boy came in. She took his dripping coat and cap, and as he moved into the firelight I saw that he was about 12 years old—and pitifully crippled.

After he caught his breath, he said, "My father tried to ring you, but your phone is dead. I came to see that you're all right."

"Thank you, John," she said, and introduced us. The wind rose, raving and screaming, battering the shutters. I told them how much I loved the drama of the storm.

"You're not scared?" John asked. I started to say no, but Mrs. McIntosh, though obviously afraid of nothing, quickly said what any boy longs to hear, "Of course she was scared, and so was I. But now we've got a mon aboot."

There was a moment's silence.

Then he rose. "I'll see that everything's snug," he said. And he hobbled out with a little swagger.

Weeks later the incident still haunted me. Why hadn't I answered his question as Mrs. McIntosh had—tenderly, imaginatively? And how often before in my life, insensitive through self-absorption, had I failed to recognize another's need? . . .

By what magic had Mrs. McIntosh transformed a crippled boy into a confident man? Had it been instinctive kindness, or deliberate? Was it compassion, tact or a combination? . . .

Looking back, I realized how often I had been helped by such hearts, how often I, too, had been exalted by a single gracious phrase or act.[3]

As parents work with children, they need this gracious heart that understands the feelings of their little ones. Jesus has this graciousness with us, as He allows us to be that "mon aboot." His "smile upon us" can transform us from a crippled boy to a confident young man.

A sensitive surgeon understood the needs "of a little boy who was devoted to a battered, one-eyed teddy bear. Hospitalized for a tonsillectomy, he was holding Teddy close when the surgeon came to his bedside just before the operation. A nurse moved to take the bear, but the doctor said gravely, 'Leave Teddy there. He needs attention, too.'

"When the child regained consciousness Teddy was snuggled against the pillow—and across his missing eye was the neatest bandage a skillful surgeon could devise."[4]

One can almost feel the Savior's love and see His smile as Sister Norma B. Ashton recounts the late Elder Marvin J. Ashton's experience at a stake conference.

"As often happens, a member of the stake presidency took Elder Ashton to greet the Primary children, who were meeting separately. [This was the procedure a number of years ago.] My husband spoke to them briefly, patted the heads of a few children sitting close to him, and left with his host to join the main body of the conference.

"As the two men were walking down the hall, they heard the running of small feet and a voice calling, 'Elder Ashton.' Marv stopped, waited for a little boy to catch up to him, and asked, 'What can I do for you?' Looking up at him with hurt in his eyes the young lad said, 'You didn't pat *my* head.' Marv gave the young man an extra pat or two and ruffled his blond hair a bit, and was rewarded as the Primary child smiled and ran back to his class.

"He gave the boy only a pat on the head, but it was just what that little person needed. The child was assured that he was just as important as those on the front row."[5]

Not only should we nurture children with thoughtful acts of kindness, as was demonstrated by Elder Ashton, but we also have the responsibility as parents to be the Savior's instruments, to teach them in truth as He did the Nephites. Elder James E. Faust said, "The Lord has a great work for each of us to do. . . . The Lord can do remarkable miracles with a person of ordinary ability who is humble, faithful, and diligent in serving . . . and seeks to improve himself."[6]

While serving as Relief Society General President I came to know firsthand many such humble, faithful sisters who were diligently teaching their children gospel truths. I saw remarkable miracles in the making. I was privileged to visit with Saints in the Philippines and found how difficult it is in some areas to obtain water. Frail young boys, sometimes undernourished, could be seen carrying buckets of water that seemed to weigh more than they did.

The water was often polluted, which resulted in an unusually high infant mortality rate. One family with whom we talked lost their first five children to dysentery. Then the parents heard the message of the gospel and joined the Church. They were taught water purification techniques by the welfare missionaries. Now they have six *healthy* children. The neighbors were amazed and began asking how they too could get a "Mormon" baby who would not succumb to hospitalization and death.

In a small village outside Manilla the homes were built on stilts. From the main road we took the dry path that led down to the hamlet. We were greeted by an energetic grandmother, who welcomed us into her living quarters. In our visit we learned that she was the matriarch of a large family. Most of the people living in this cluster of houses were her descendants. One of her sons was the bishop of their ward.

Though her dwelling was small and scantily furnished, it was absolutely clean and orderly. At the far end of the one-room unit was a table with a dishpan. Standing next to that was a clearly labeled bottle of bleach. Near the couch, where we sat, was a large chalkboard leaning against the wall on which the formula for water purification was neatly printed. She was clearly prepared to present a lesson, which she did regularly. She wanted her children and her grandchildren to know what she knew.

After we had had a nice visit, learning about her family and interests, this diminutive woman, no taller than my shoulder, half running, half skipping to keep up, accompanied us up the dusty pathway to the road. She wanted to be sure we knew of her newfound joy in the knowledge of the gospel and the life-saving health principles she had been taught. Having learned these wonderful truths she did all she could to share. Her countenance glowed with the love of Christ as she enthusiastically told me, "Sister Winder, I teach! I teach! I teach!"

This wonderful Filipino mother in her humble circumstances was following the pattern the Savior set, to teach those around her. Another righteous mother, Lucy Mack Smith, not only taught her children verbally, but also by her example of quietly and consistently incorporating righteous principles into her everyday living. Elder Marvin J. Ashton once asked, "Have you ever wondered what inspired [the Prophet] to turn to prayer when he was troubled and doubting?"

> Lucy, Joseph's mother, had planted the seeds. From an early age she depended on prayer for guidance and strength. . . . "I determined to obtain that which I had heard spoken so much of from the pulpit—a change of heart. To accomplish this I spent much of my time reading the Bible and praying."
>
> Later in her life Lucy was seriously troubled by the fact that she could not get her husband, Joseph Sr., to join with her in attending religious meetings. When all of her invitations and persuasion failed, she resorted to another measure. This was something she often did and of which her children were very much aware. She made her desires, anxieties, and frustrations known to her Heavenly Father in prayer. She writes that she "*retired to a grove not far distant,* where I prayed to the Lord in behalf of my husband—that the *true gospel* might be presented to him and that his heart might be softened so as to receive it, or, that he might become more religiously inclined." . . . When the gospel of Jesus Christ was restored, Joseph's father became a valiant member. He believed Joseph before he believed the gospel. The prayers of a mother were answered through the prayer of a son. If Lucy had not effectively taught that great family lesson, would Joseph have "retired to the grove"? . . .
>
> A love of God and the unwavering knowledge of God's existence were part of Joseph's education in a spiritual home. These traits were not taught by lectures or scolding. Visual aids were ever present. Joseph saw his parents kneeling in prayer; he knew his mother went to a grove to petition the Lord; he felt the love of the Lord in his home. The family read the Bible, sang hymns, and discussed the scriptures together. Religious conduct was not a weekend activity. It was a way of daily life.[7]

How the Lord must have smiled on this valiant family, even as He did upon the steadfast Nephites!

I saw the Savior's pattern work for me on that Primary day many years ago when my smile gave little Jamie confidence, acceptance, and a feeling of being loved. It helped prepare him to be taught the gospel truths. I recognized my responsibility to teach and nurture him and other children, as the Savior had done for the Nephites when "his countenance did smile upon them."

NOTES

1. Boyd K. Packer, "Reverence Invites Revelation," *Ensign,* November 1991, p. 22.

2. Gordon B. Hinckley, "Live Worthy of the Girl You Will Someday Marry," *Ensign,* May 1998, p. 50.

3. Elizabeth Byrd, "Rewards of a Gracious Heart," *Readers Digest* (Pleasantville, New York: Readers Digest Association, Inc., 1971), pp. 106–7.

4. Ibid., p. 108.

5. Norma Ashton, "A Unique Melody," *Ensign,* September 1989, p. 27.

6. James E. Faust, "Acting for Ourselves and Not Being Acted Upon," *Ensign,* November 1995, p. 45.

7. Marvin J. Ashton, "I Went Home" (Salt Lake City: Deseret Book, 1980), pp. 3–5.

Chapter Six

Happiness Intended

"Be of good cheer."
—3 Nephi 1:13

by
Karen J. Ashton

Nothing I had ever heard or read had prepared me for the physical and emotional intensity of motherhood. Physically, there was no rest. I had a new sympathy for the little robin outside my window who was forever feeding and warming her young.

"Successful marriages and families are established and maintained on principles of faith, prayer, repentance, forgiveness, respect, love, compassion, work, and wholesome recreational activities."

The Family: A Proclamation to the World

*M*OMENTS AFTER MY FIRST BABY'S birth they placed her in my arms. As I touched her tiny fingers I laughed and cried at the same time. She was beautiful! She opened her eyes and looked, for the first time, at the mortal world she was now a part of. I was seeing a brand new world myself. I was looking through the eyes of a mother. The pathway of life ahead of me, which had seemed to contain so many choices moments ago, had suddenly straightened out. Someone else's life and well-being depended on me. There would be no skydiving lessons, speedboat racing, or any other high-risk adventures. I prayed I would be equal to the responsibility. I was determined to be the best mother, homemaker, housekeeper, hostess, Saint, and citizen the world had ever seen.

The windows of heaven opened over the next few years and it rained babies. By the time Emily was three we had two other children and a good case of reality had set in. There were dishes, diapers, earaches, doctors, errands, and meals. That doesn't begin to mention the weightier responsibilities of teaching my little ones the gospel and being a worthy example. Nothing I had ever heard or read had prepared me for the physical and emotional intensity of motherhood. Physically, there was no rest. I had a new sympathy for the little robin outside my window who was forever feeding and warming her young. Emotionally, huge roots of love had grown into and around my heart. I knew that if something were to hurt my children or suddenly take them from me I would bleed uncontrollably. I loved my children as I had never loved anything or anyone in my life. Even when I managed to get away, the anxiety for their well-being would

KAREN J. ASHTON and her husband, Alan, are the parents of eleven children and thirteen grandchildren. She has served on the Primary General Board, is the founder of the Timpanogos Storytelling Festival, and sits on the boards of Governors for the Utah Shakespearean Festival, the Brigham Young University Museum of Art, and the Foundation of Primary Children's Medical Center.

thunder over me like a herd of elephants. Frankly, I was exhausted.

One morning, I called my mother and cried: "I'm so tired. I'm going to die!" Her reply was short and to the point. "Get used to it. You're going to feel that way the rest of your life." I was stunned by her blunt and seemingly uncaring remark. Later that day I happened to relate my mother's comment to another young mother. I couldn't believe it. She laughed! Then, to my surprise, I laughed too. Neither of us questioned the truth of what my mother had said. Somehow, laughing about it brought relief and broke the tension and fatigue I had been feeling all morning.

Because parenthood is the highest and holiest of callings, it's easy to feel overwhelmed with the responsibility and forget to enjoy the process. The Lord wants us to be happy and find joy in our work as well as joy and rejoicing in our posterity. Understanding God's love for us and for our children should fill us with hope, happiness, and good cheer.

The Lord has said, "In the world ye shall have tribulation" but "be of good cheer; I have overcome the world" (John 16:33). The atonement of the Lord Jesus Christ brings "good tidings of great joy" (Luke 2:10) for all people. The gospel is the good news. As parents, we can look to the scriptures for reassurance, balance, and hope: "Lift up your hearts and be glad, for I am in your midst, and am your advocate with the Father; and it is his good will to give you the kingdom" (D&C 29:5). "Be glad in the Lord, and rejoice, ye righteous: and shout for joy, all ye that are upright in heart" (Psalm 32:11). "And thou shalt rejoice in every good thing which the Lord thy God hath given thee" (Deuteronomy 26:11). "Happy art thou, O Israel: who is like unto thee, O people saved by the Lord" (Deuteronomy 33:29). "Be of good cheer, for I will lead you along. The kingdom is yours and the blessings thereof are yours, and the riches of eternity are yours" (D&C 78:18).

Over the years I have come across some very practical steps that help me be of good cheer and find joy and rejoicing in the process of parenthood. Even during the most trying times with one's children, "a [cheerful] heart doeth good like a medicine" (Proverbs 17:22).

Count your blessings. It's hard to remain downcast or overwhelmed when you realize how blessed you are. I believe it is impossible to feel both gratitude and gloom at the same time. Our Heavenly Father has given us "every good thing" (Deuteronomy 26:11; Moroni 7:22). He wants us to be successful. We have living prophets to guide us, the Holy Ghost to inspire us, scriptures to enlighten us, priesthood to bless us, and covenants to reassure us. If we remain faithful we have the Lord's assurance that "ye shall have eternal life" (2 Nephi 31:20). This knowledge should make us the most optimistic, hopeful, cheerful people on the face of the earth. We can go forward with faith, enjoying all that is good in the process.

Laugh at yourself. The recognition of your own imperfections is a sign of humility. Expecting perfection of yourself can lead to discouragement and depression. You will make mistakes. The hope is you will learn from them.

After breast-feeding my firstborn for three months I was anxious to begin feeding her solids. My doctor said I could feed her rice cereal and maybe some bottled bananas. I was so excited! (New mothers can't repress the desire to see their little one leap to the next stage of development.) Now, I thought, if bottled bananas were good for her, fresh bananas would be better, right? So at every meal I fed her fresh mashed bananas. After about two weeks something was terribly wrong. Her plumbing was stuck big time. Poor baby! I called the doctor. Oh, my goodness! I'd fed her the wrong thing! It seems fresh bananas cause constipation. Grief! *Guilt!* After the problem moved along I had a good laugh over my own ignorance.

Understand who your children really are. The words of a well-known Christmas hymn remind me not only of the Savior's birth but of the birth of every new child of God into the world.

> How silently, how silently
> The wondrous gift is giv'n!
> So God imparts to human hearts
> The blessings of his heav'n.
> ("Oh Little Town of Bethlehem," *Hymns,* no. 208).

Little children come from the presence of God the Father clean, whole, innocent (see Moroni 8:8), and full of potential. In his "Intimations of Immortality" the poet Wordsworth said it so well: "Trailing clouds of glory do we come from God, who is our home."

Following the Savior's death and resurrection in Jerusalem, He visited the Nephites on the American continent. With great compassion He blessed the sick and afflicted. He prayed for the multitude, using words that "no tongue can speak, neither can there be written by any man." The Savior then took the little children, "one by one, and blessed them, and prayed unto the Father for them" (3 Nephi 17:21). "Behold your little ones," He commanded. The heavens opened, angels descended, and fire encircled those little ones. Angels ministered to the children (see 3 Nephi 17:24). Undoubtedly the parents of these children gained a new perspective about their children's place and potential in the kingdom of God. Certainly they understood the Savior's love for the little ones. That generation of children remained faithful, as also did their children and many of their grandchildren.

We should "pray unto the Father always in [the Savior's] name that [our] . . . children may be blessed" (3 Nephi 18:21), that they may have ministering angels in times of need and that they may remain faithful. As parents we should plead to behold our little ones with an eternal perspective.

It has always been amusing to me to realize that my children are teaching me as much as or more than I will ever teach them. Their presence in my home has helped me learn the demanding lessons of patience, humility, endurance, long-suffering, love unfeigned, and kindness. Often I have felt they understand more than they can speak. Certainly, "little children do have words given unto them many times, which confound the wise and the learned" (Alma 32:23).

Years ago my husband and I built our dream home. It was wonderful! We finally had room for our family of thirteen. After moving in I began to purchase prints and paintings I thought would help us remember the Lord and invite the Spirit into our home.

One evening my husband and I were admiring a painting of the First Vision by Floyd Brynholt that had just arrived. We had placed it above the mantel in our living room. As we stood there, our tiny daughter, three-year-old Rebekah, walked up next to us. With a tone of familiarity and love that made the hair on the back of my neck stand up, she said, "It's Joseph." Her little face was aglow with recognition. You can believe it was very quiet in the room for several moments. She turned and left just as quickly as she had come. My husband and I looked at each other. I whispered, "Have you been talking to her about the Prophet Joseph or the First Vision?" He shook his head. He asked me the same question. Sadly I admitted I hadn't either.

When things don't go well, take a step back from the situation. Regain perspective. Sin is the greatest cause for concern in our children's lives. All other concerns fall somewhere behind. Remember that little children "cannot sin" (D&C 29:47). As a parent you have been given many years in which Satan is unable to tempt your children. The Lord says that He has done this "that great things may be required at the hand of their fathers" (D&C 29:48). Could it be that some of these "great things" are: love, long-suffering, kindness, unselfishness (see Moroni 7:45), gentleness, forgiveness, patience, and instruction? (see D&C 68:25–28). This is an unparalleled time to lovingly teach, guide, and reinforce proper behavior. Being harsh with little children is inappropriate.

Your personal worthiness puts you in a position to be prompted by the Holy Ghost. Listen carefully. Trust your feelings and thoughts. When you pray, remember each child individually and their specific needs. When reproof is necessary, give it as soon as you notice the misbehavior. Focus directly on the misbehavior. Don't attack the child. Afterwards, show forth greater love (see D&C 121:43).

Even after children reach the age of accountability they are more likely to make mistakes or show lack of judgment than commit sins. Backing the car into the neighbor's tree is a mistake, not a sin. Leaving homework to the last minute is a misjudgment, not a sin.

Your ability to lead and guide your children will depend a great deal on the relationship of love you have developed. As you counsel and comfort your children, remember your own youth. Were you perfect? Did you make mistakes? Remembering will help put your child's mistakes in perspective. Share with your children the mistakes you made and what you learned from them. It's certainly good for a few laughs.

The day Amy Jo, my second daughter, got her driver's licence, she begged to be able to take her younger brothers and sisters to 7-Eleven for a treat. I consented. I cautioned her that backing out of the small 7-

Eleven parking lot with our fifteen-passenger van would be very difficult. I suggested that a trip to the neighborhood grocery store might be better. She smiled, shook her head at my lack of confidence, and left.

She returned in tears thirty minutes later. "I backed into the Flemings' car," she whispered.

I smiled. "That's not a very funny joke, Amy Jo."

"It's not a joke," she sobbed.

My heart sank. She had not taken my counsel. She had, in fact, backed into my best friend's car at 7-Eleven. I was stunned! I had warned her! Was this disobedience? Certainly it was irresponsibility! I tried to calm down and remember a time when I had been irresponsible with a car. It didn't take long. As a young woman I had repeatedly ignored the blinking oil light in our old '54 Ford. While I was traveling down the freeway one day the engine froze up. There was a sudden clunking sound, then black smoke. Sigh! No more engine. No more car. After replaying my own experience I was able to be more understanding with my daughter.

Project forward. When things don't go exactly as you would wish, or when there is a minor tragedy, don't let anger take over. Pause for a moment and find the humor in the situation. Think how you are going to tell this story in ten years' time. Remember that crisis plus time equals humor. When you project forward like this you can actually enjoy the humor up front. You also store it in a humor bank where you can take it out and laugh over and over again.

One morning I found the name "Spencer" written in black crayon over my son Spencer's bed. I marched down to the family room, confronted five-year-old Spencer, and demanded to know why he would do such a thing! He looked up at me for a moment and then asked, "How did you know it was me?"

I could hardly keep from laughing. "Because you wrote your name," I answered with a smile. It took both of us several minutes to scrub his name off the wall. The very next morning I discovered the name "Bat Man" written in the same place. As I stared at the wall I couldn't help but shake my head and smile at the thought process of a five-year-old. I knew this was going to make a great story. In fact, I told it at his wedding breakfast not long ago. By the way, Spencer did scrub the wall again.

Sometimes it takes time to see the humor in a situation, particularly when you're the one who makes the mistake. My son Morgan was chosen to be Santa Claus in his first-grade Christmas program. Such an honor! I was eight months pregnant with our eighth child and had my hands full with two little preschoolers. I stayed up until 2:00 A.M. sewing his costume. As he ran out to the bus stop the next morning, he yelled, "Don't forget, Mom. The program is at 1:00."

I replied, "Me forget? Never! I wouldn't miss it for anything. You're going to be the best Santa ever. I can't wait to hear your Ho Ho Ho."

At eleven o'clock I put my two preschoolers down for a nap. I thought, "If I'm lucky, they might sleep until twelve." I woke up at 1:20! By the time I got to the school with my two little ones in tow there were no cars in the parking lot. Bad sign! When I reached the school library, Morgan was sitting alone on a chair in the middle of the room. All the other mothers had taken their children home right after the program. His little body was slumped forward. The Santa beard I had made the night before was hanging from one hand. His eyes were trained on his little black boots. The thought that I had inflicted pain on my own son stabbed at me. Kneeling in front of his chair I broke into tears. I pleaded with him to forgive me. I told him it had been a terrible mistake. He turned away from me. Great sobs now shook my body. One of my little preschoolers started patting my back in an attempt to comfort me. Suddenly, I could hear someone else in the room crying. It was Morgan's teacher. She begged him to forgive me. He only turned further away. Finally, when there were no more tears, I stood, gathered my preschoolers and Morgan's backpack, and started out to the car. Luckily he followed. There was no laughing that day.

Years later Morgan was running for high school student body vice president. We stayed up night after night working on posters, assemblies, and campaign buttons as well as entertaining fellow candidates. On the night that the election results were to be announced, both of us were exhausted. He left early for a candidate dinner. I refused to take a nap for fear I would miss the announcement dance.

Later that evening my husband and I sat on the high school bleachers waiting. As each new officer was announced, a cheer arose from the students assembled. The new officer would then come to the front and accept his position. Finally it was time. The speaker blared out, "Vice President for 1991—Morgan Ashton!" Everyone cheered. Morgan did not come to the front. Three times they called his name. I was sick! Where could he be? Suddenly, I knew.

My husband and I drove home and I ran downstairs to his room. When I opened the door I could see two big feet sticking out from the bottom of the bed. He had slept through the announcement. Apparently he had come home after the dinner and slipped downstairs for a little nap. I shook his foot, "You won, Morgan. You won!"

He groaned, then bolted upright. "No! No! I didn't miss it!"

"I'm so sorry," I said sincerely. "It was wonderful. Everyone cheered for you . . . three times."

Now he was really awake and in agony. "Oh, no!" He groaned.

I felt so sad for him. I confess, however, that images of his first-grade program were dancing through my mind.

"There is something I need you to know," I said.

"What?" he asked.

Relieved, after *years* of guilt, I proudly stated, "I WAS THERE!"

I really do believe that sooner or later a mother who is doing her best has the last laugh.

Have fun together. "The Family: A Proclamation to the World" states: "Successful marriages and families are established and maintained on principles of faith, prayer, repentance, forgiveness, respect, love, compassion, work, and wholesome recreational activities." Shared experiences and common memories bond families together. Successful family activities don't just happen. They are the result of planning, effort, and love (usually on the part of the mother). Every lesson you try to teach in your family will go better if you include a good measure of fun. As Mary Poppins said, "A spoonful of sugar makes the medicine go down."

Our earliest family home evenings always included at least four rousing renditions of "Ring Around the Rosie." Emily looked forward to having both Mommy and Daddy play with her before we had the lesson.

Family vacations are the best! Plan carefully and plan together. Anticipation is part of the fun. Keep the travel time down and the fun time up. Remember that parents like to "see" but children like to "do." Let your children have your undivided attention. Play together. Families who have fun together are blessed over and over. They are blessed while they participate in the fun and also each and every time they enjoy the memory. Our family has laughed and laughed over the many times we were stranded in our old motor home. (Remember, crisis plus time equals humor.) We all know the inside jokes from our trips to Lake Powell. We all joke about who the best game player is. We love a puzzle on a snowy winter day. Please! Whatever you do, don't miss out on the fun!

Love, love, love, love, love your children. The word *love* appears five times in "The Family: A Proclamation to the World." I certainly understand why. No one—*no one* gets too much. Most of us would like just a little more. It is as important to us as the food we eat or the air we breathe. I've never heard anyone complain that they get too much love. The Savior's admonition to "love one another" (John 13:34, 35) certainly applies to the family.

It's easy to hug and kiss little children. Sometimes we forget that as children grow into adulthood they need a good deal of affection as well. Years ago I became concerned that I had stopped hugging and kissing my older children. I made a decision to start again. The first time I hugged my sixteen-year-old son he froze up like a block of ice. His response let me know that it had been way too long between hugs. I felt bad, but I decided to keep trying. I am pleased to be able to tell you that now I can hug my older children and they hug me back. I love it!

Loving relationships take time. There are those who believe a loving relationship can be developed by giving highly concentrated attention for short periods of time (quality time). That is a little like saying you can bake a cake just as well at 500 degrees for eight minutes as you can at 350 degrees for thirty minutes. Children need the constant warming of love over a long period of time. Give them your attention. Tell them how much you love them. Tell them how wonderful they are. Be available when they need you. Make time for your children. Some things cannot be rushed. Love is one of them.

The windows of heaven remained open for us. By the end of the baby downpour we had had eleven children in sixteen years. To that number we have since added five wonderful spouses and thirteen grandchildren. I still feel a tremendous stretching to meet the demands of family. As a family, we have known our share of sorrow. We have also enjoyed an abundance of laughter, love, fun, happiness, and good cheer. The gospel has been our sure foundation. I "have no greater joy than to hear that my children walk in truth" (3 John 1:4). Now I understand what joy and rejoicing is. My children are some of my best friends. I can never repay the Lord for His love and for the incredible opportunity to be a parent. Life is wonderful! Enjoy it!

CHAPTER SEVEN

Avoid Anger: A Winning Way

"And blessed are ye if ye have no
disputations among you."
—3 NEPHI 18:34

by
Janet Thomas

The key to easing the sting of disputes that will come in family life is that generosity of spirit, a willingness to accommodate a different viewpoint or to allow experience to teach without having to have the last word.

"It is Abraham who took the initiative and said unto Lot, 'Let there be no strife, I pray thee, between me and thee . . .' The complete, genuine willingness of Abraham to adjust to whatever Lot's decision was is the mark of a generosity of spirit of that remarkable patriarch."

NEAL A. MAXWELL

*A*S A CHILD GROWING UP IN MY PARENTS' home, and even as an adult, I never remember my father yelling. He simply never expressed his anger or displeasure in this way. I know now that this trait was an attribute of his nature as well as a conscious choice. But simply not hearing loud voices raised in argument in our home has had a profound influence in the lives of my brothers and sisters and me.

I have a clear memory of one incident that happened when I was about seven in which my father taught me by his example and let me learn from my experience.

It was a gusty spring day and my father had brought home a kite for us to fly. Being the oldest, I assumed that the kite was mine. We were in the front yard, and the kite was flying high above the neighboring homes. The string was played out nearly to the end. We were having a wonderful time, but the wind that was keeping the kite aloft also blew in a few dark clouds. In the distance I heard a faint clap of thunder. Then, a very few raindrops fell.

I panicked. I had visions of my beautiful paper kite soaked and ruined. I had vaguely heard about Benjamin Franklin and his kite being hit by lightning. Suddenly, I had to get my kite down now! I started pulling the string in without taking time to wind it, letting it gather in a tangled heap at my feet.

My dad tried to reason with me. He told me that the rain was so light it wouldn't hurt my kite. He asked me to wind the string around the cardboard holder so that it wouldn't become tangled.

JANET THOMAS received a master's in English from Brigham Young University and has worked as a writer and producer for radio, television, and advertising. She is currently an editor at The New Era *magazine. She has served as a Relief Society president and teacher, as a stake Young Women president, and is now the Beehive advisor in her ward.*

I was beyond reason. I couldn't put my fears into words. In fact, I'm not sure I knew enough to verbalize what was frightening me. I just had to get that kite down immediately.

Instead of yelling at me, grabbing the string out of my hands, or shoving me aside, Dad let me pull the kite in, tangled string and all. As soon as the kite was on the ground, it became clear that what my father had told me was true. My kite was fine. It was not wet, torn, or burned. But the string was a hopeless mess, a mess I had created unnecessarily. If I had listened to my father I could still have had my kite with a usable string that could be flown again. I remember realizing even at that early age that what my father had told me was right and that it would have been better for me if I had done what he told me.

My father's example of avoiding an angry display taught me more vividly than any other method. In his book, *That My Family Should Partake,* Elder Neal A. Maxwell says, "Our children, seeing the sermon of our actual behavior (more than hearing what we say), are bound to make their own assessment of our relationship as parents. John Donne wrote: 'The subsequent life is the best printing and the most useful and profitable publishing of a Sermon.' "[1]

I know now that this would be the lifelong pattern my father would use to teach his children. He would tell us the truth about a situation and what he thought we ought to do about it. Then when we made a decision he would not fly into a rage when we did not follow his guidance or advice. He would never even say, "I told you so," when the result would be exactly as disastrous as he anticipated. He was there to ask us what we thought of our experience, sincerely, and with no anger. He was also there to pick up the pieces. We soon learned that it was a very good thing to follow Dad's advice. Anger was useless and got us nowhere.

THE DAMAGE THAT CAN BE DONE

On a radio program, with commentary on the family, I heard the following story given by Dr. James C. Dobson.

Many parents, perhaps the majority, admit to losing their tempers and screaming at their kids from time to time. Usually we shrug it off assuming that not much harm was done. But is that really the case?

Deep in the woods of the Solomon Islands lives a tribe of villagers who practice a strange form of logging. When a tree is too large to be felled with an axe, they bring it down by yelling at it. Tribesmen believed to have special powers sneak up on the tree at dawn and scream at the top of their lungs. Day after day, they repeat this practice. Eventually the tree dies and falls to the ground. "It kills the spirit of the tree," they say.

Well, I'll admit that I'm a bit skeptical of this practice and that it works on trees, but I'll tell you this much, it will sure bring down a human being. If you want to kill someone's spirit, yelling is a great way to get it done. And no spirit on earth is more fragile than that of a child. Though we mean no harm when we scream and shout at our kids, there's nothing harmless about it. It's humiliating, and it's discouraging to children, and it often leaves scars that will last for a lifetime.[2]

When I heard this little story I had two reactions. Much like Dr. Dobson, I sincerely doubt that this is a legitimate or viable way of logging trees. It seems a little far-fetched that trees could die just by having someone yell at them. But I also felt that there was some truth to the story. Yelling does cause damage. Expressed anger hurts. And something inside does die.

JUSTICE FOR ALL

For most of my life, my father served as a district judge. He arbitrated disputes nearly every day. To help us understand what he did, he used to bring home the briefs and law books pertaining to some of his cases. He told us the facts of the case, then had us read a little bit about the precedents set by other courts on cases with similar circumstances. Then he would ask us what we would decide if we were the judge.

I remember one simple case in particular. It seems some cattle had been placed in a rented pasture. The owner of the pasture had neglected the upkeep on the fence. The cows got out and one was hit and killed, badly damaging a car. The owner of the car was suing.

There were all sorts of interesting details. In a rural state like the one we lived in, a cow has as much right-of-way on a road as a car. The owner of the pasture was being paid to care for the cows and had an obligation to keep the fence in good repair so the cows could not get out. And the owner of the cow is reponsible for the damage his animal causes. After we stewed over the case, we concluded that the plaintiff was suing the wrong person. We triumphantly told Dad that they should just start over. But then he pointed out that each lawsuit must be worked through to a conclusion. Once a suit was filed, the machinery of the courts was put in motion; there had to be an orderly resolution.

Then Dad taught us a great lesson about disputes. We asked the reason that these men were in court over a rather straightforward matter, where each person should accept some responsibility and some of the financial burden. Dad said, "They come to court because they can't work it out among themselves."

I remember realizing the value of being reasonable, accepting responsibility, and even bending over backward for someone else, lessons my parents tried to teach their own children.

I also attended Dad's court and watched the sentencing of those caught breaking laws. I saw that the demands of justice had to be met. Often those being sentenced to jail would bluster and argue, making excuses for their actions, asking that they be made the exception. My father would calmly listen to them and then pass sentence.

When Dad got home after court, then I would corner him and ask about what I had seen. "Dad," I would ask, "didn't you feel a little sorry for that guy?"

My father would then explain about the law, that certain penalties accompanied certain crimes. It wasn't the judge who decided how much time each lawbreaker would spend in jail; it was the penalty phase of the law. Dad explained that his feelings had very little to do with it. If a person was found guilty, then a penalty was attached. That was what was meant by the demands of justice. Society had rules. When the laws were broken, the penalty applied.

All his life Dad worried how mercy could temper justice. He pored over the scriptures in Alma. And in small ways, rather imaginative ways, he tried to temper the penalty that the law demanded. For example, once two teens were brought to Dad's court having been caught vandalizing some buildings and machinery on a dry farm some distance from town. The two boys, just barely of adult age, had caused thousands of dollars worth of damage, particularly to the machinery. Because of the high dollar amount of the damage and their recent adult status, the boys were charged with felonies. Confessing their guilt, the boys were now brought before the judge to receive their penalty.

Understanding the devastating effect a criminal record could have on the rest of their lives, the young men were truly remorseful and humble, willing to do whatever it took to rectify their crime. With the cooperation of the other law enforcement agencies, Dad sentenced these young men to the shortest jail time possible on the condition that they remain on probation while they worked and paid back the farmer for the damage that was done to his property. The boys were to reimburse the farmer not just the amount of the damage, but twice the amount. The other condition of their punishment was that the boys had to find jobs and pay back the double amount themselves. They could not accept help from their parents or anyone else. If they completed their penalty with exactness, then their criminal record would be wiped clean. There would be no permanent record of the event. They could then go on to serve in the Church, vote, enter business, and have other freedoms that go with a clear record.

I have often thought of that penalty. In many ways it would have been easier and cheaper for the young men to simply sit out their time in jail, without making restitution. But Dad knew the steps of repentance. As a judge, he did not have unlimited freedom to change the penalty. But he could offer them a chance to make restitution in such a way that if they chose to truly repent they would know that they had done everything possible. They would have confidence that they had gone beyond what was required, the extra mile, so to speak. Through humbly accepting the atonement of Christ and making restitution, they could have the burden of their sin lifted completely. They could meet that farmer on the streets and both he and they would know that they had made amends as far as it was possible for them to do. The lives of these young men would not be adversely affected in any long-term way, because they had chosen a higher law.

All of sudden, I realized that this was mercy—to offer a way for those young men to truly rid themselves of the burden of sin.

How does this apply to a family? A wise parent has to allow his children to feel the consequences of their poor choices having to do with the rules of the family. But when the penalty can also offer the child a chance to feel redeemed, mercy enters in.

Anger Between Siblings

Children will argue. My siblings and I certainly did, even though we had fine examples in our parents of avoiding anger. But we were carefully taught that arguing did little to get us what we wanted.

One thing my parents did to counteract the damaging effects of competition among their children was to play lots of games with us. My father loved buying board games, looking carefully for those that seemed clever and fun. Both my parents loved playing games and made it enjoyable, cheering when someone made a good move and moaning when someone slipped up. But they made it very clear that playing the game together was more important than who won.

They didn't, however, make the mistake of not keeping score or not trying hard. That too was taught, just like good work ethics. You always tried to do your best at the game. However, when one child won, the game did not stop. That child was simply the *first* winner. The game continued until someone else finished. He or she was the *second* winner. If the game could continue, then it did until we had a *third, fourth, fifth,* and *last* winner. Dad even used those labels. We were "first winner," "second winner," and so on to "last winner." It was always thrilling to be winner, even if I completed the game a little later than everyone else.

This way of playing games spoke volumes. We were encouraged to compete because it was fun. Yes, we needed to strive to win. But winning itself was just the result of the game. This time I might win, but next time my brother might win. We played lots and lots of games and learned to cheer for another's success and graciously accept winning or losing. It was the playing together that became important.

It seems ironic that playing a lot of competitive games taught us how to avoid being competitive with each other.

WE'LL BE THERE

Another thing my parents encouraged that I know reduced friction among my brothers and sisters was our going to each other's events. When my brother played his little league baseball games, we were there. When I was participating in a speech festival, my brothers and sisters were in the audience with my parents. Whenever one of us had a musical recital, we all went trooping in. We were all there as a family for each child's success or failure. It was just expected that if one of us was involved in something, everyone else would be there. It gave us confidence because we knew we had a support near at hand. And it helped ease the discouraging times, because we also knew we had a group that cared, no matter what.

HE'S YOUR BROTHER

Sometimes arguments don't have good resolutions. The argument may involve a whole range of grays instead of black and white. The whole idea that you need to have someone admit that they are wrong before a dispute can be resolved is foolish in a family or in life. There is nothing to be gained by simply being right at the expense of a brother or sister. We are all in these things together.

In a sense, this is the feeling that my parents promoted. Supporting a brother or sister was more important than being right. Of course, I am talking about relatively simple childhood arguments that carried no dark overtones of something more seriously amiss in the lives of family members.

We saw a perfect example in our father's relationships with his own precious brothers. He would do anything for them, as they would for him. None would dream of taking unfair or undeserved advantage of the others. My father explained that this feeling was nurtured by their mother. Whenever her sons would argue, as children will do, she would turn to each in turn and say, "But he's your brother." After that, trying to win the argument seemed so much less worthy than simply trying to make amends.

The scriptures are full of family relationships at their best and at their worst. One of the best is illustrated in the relationship between

Abraham and his nephew Lot. Elder Neal A. Maxwell made this comment about what could have been an opportunity for discord. "We see generosity of spirit in the life of Abraham when he and Lot, who was his nephew, found their cattle grazing on the same land. There was strife between the herdsmen of Abraham's cattle and of Lot's cattle. It is Abraham who took the initiative and said unto Lot, 'Let there be no strife, I pray thee, between me and thee, and between my herdmen and thy herdmen; for we be brethren. Is not the whole land before thee? separate thyself, I pray thee, from me; if thou wilt take the left hand, then I will go to the right; or if thou depart to the right hand, then I will go to the left.' (Genesis 13:7–9.) The complete, genuine willingness of Abraham to adjust to whatever Lot's decision was is the mark of a generosity of spirit of that remarkable patriarch."[3]

The key to easing the sting of disputes that will come in family life is that generosity of spirit, a willingness to accommodate a different viewpoint or to allow experience to teach without having to have the last word. Children will learn this by example from their parents. As I watched my father avoid anger, I learned to control my own volatile childish temper. And when anger is removed from the equation, then solutions can be found to satisfy all sides.

NOTES

1. Neal A. Maxwell, *That My Family Should Partake* (Salt Lake City: Deseret Book, 1974), p. 70.

2. James C. Dobson, "Screaming at Trees and Children," *Focus on the Family Commentary,* April 24, 1998.

3. Neal A. Maxwell, *That My Family Should Partake*, pp. 92–93.

in Anger

1. Don't power struggle

2. interview the other person

3. Don't talk down to spouse — as a parent to child —

ie:

Only use parent-child communication in kids under 8.

CHAPTER EIGHT

The Safety of the Rock

"And the winds blew and beat upon
that house and it fell not, for it was
founded upon a rock."
—3 NEPHI 14:25

by
Joy F. Evans

*Our own example of patience and trust and endurance when
"the winds blow" will likely be of the greatest help to our children when they have their personal trials.*

"No matter how serious the trial, how deep the distress, how great the affliction, God will never desert us. He never has, and He never will."

GEORGE Q. CANNON

*W*HAT ARE THE WINDS TO WHICH THE Savior refers? What is He teaching us? Beyond the natural disasters that come to mind (and they can be terrifying and devastating—raging floods, mud-soaked hillsides, tornadoes, and hurricanes) that so often kill or injure people, damage or destroy homes and farms and even whole communities, the Lord is telling us that loss and suffering might come at any time to anyone of us. We have never been promised that the "winds and rain and floods" will not beat upon our houses, but rather have been assured that we can endure adversity and grief and challenge if our "house" is built upon the rock of Jesus Christ. When we know that Jesus is the Christ, when our faith is strong and sure, when we are obedient to the principles of the gospel, then our "house" can stand, whatever our challenges.

And surely each of us will have challenges! This may not seem to us to be "fair" when we are trying to do all the right things, but we can know—and this surely—that, as the Lord taught Joseph Smith at a time of terrible trial, "all these things shall give thee experience, and shall be for thy good" (D&C 122:7).

"Beloved, think it not strange concerning the fiery trial which is to try you, as though some strange thing happened unto you" (1 Peter 4:12).

"And now . . . I would that ye should remember, that as much as ye shall put your trust in God even so much ye shall be delivered out of your trials, and your troubles, and your afflictions, and ye shall be lifted up at the last day" (Alma 38:5).

Do the scriptures tell us, also, that even little children can have

---

Joy F. Evans and her husband, David C. Evans, with their ten children and one Apache daughter, have thirty-six grandchildren and a great-granddaughter. Joy is a registered nurse and a graduate of the University of Utah. She has served as a member of the Relief Society General Board and as first counselor to Barbara W. Winder in the general presidency.

personal challenges? "Jacob . . . my first-born . . . in the wilderness
. . . in thy childhood thou hast suffered afflictions and much sorrow.
. . . Nevertheless . . . thou knowest the greatness of God; and he shall
consecrate thine afflictions for thy gain" (2 Nephi 2:1, 2).

Our own example of patience and trust and endurance when "the
winds blow" will likely be of the greatest help to our children when
they have their personal trials. The hope is that our consistent efforts
to teach them to pray and to walk uprightly, to have faith, to keep the
commandments, will become such a part of their very beings that
they can, indeed, suffer sorrow and affliction with trust and patience,
even as did young Jacob. Through our own difficulties we and our
children can also come to greater understanding of and reliance upon
the Savior and the Father of us all, as George Q. Cannon once counseled the Saints when they were suffering great persecution: "No matter how serious the trial, how deep the distress, how great the affliction, [God] will never desert us. He never has, and He never will."[1]

When we truly understand this wonderful promise, we can better endure our own distresses and help our children and our other
loved ones endure theirs.

A dear friend, knowing of a special trial our family was experiencing, sent me a note with a poem enclosed that in turn had been
given to her at a time of special need. The note said:

A neighbor brought this to me when our son-in-law was so sick. She
simply gave me a hug and handed me this little verse, which she said
had been enormously helpful to her. It was the act almost as much as
the poem that touched me and gave me energy and courage.

> I shall know why, when Time is over,
> And I have ceased to wonder why;
> Christ will explain each separate anguish
> In the fair schoolroom of the sky.
>
> He will tell me what Peter promised,
> And I, for wonder at his woe,
> I shall forget the drop of Anguish
> That scalds me now, that scalds me now!
>   (Emily Dickinson)

Sometimes our suffering is "scalding" when the winds blow, but the promise of the scriptures is sure, and the love of friends helps us as they "lift up the hands which hang down, and strengthen the feeble knees" (D&C 81:5).

Sometimes our children's problems are their own, and sometimes they suffer because of being part of the family when another is hurting, for whatever reason. When our children have trials, we can listen; we can be there; sometimes we can answer their questions:

"Is Robbie going to die, Dad?"

"Why did old Rover have to get hit by a car? Will Dad bring him back from the vet? Do dogs go to heaven, Mom?"

"Mrs. Ellet, your baby is almost perfect, but he does have a serious problem. He has Down's syndrome. There will be very good resources to help you . . ."

"We've given every test—medical, psychological, physical—and the evidence strongly suggests that your husband has progressive Alzheimer's disease. The only really sure diagnosis is made by examination of the brain cells themselves at autopsy."

Are there answers to these questions and stormy situations? Where do we find them? Sometimes they are found in the scriptures, sometimes in the experiences of other people who have met similar problems, sometimes in our own experiences, sometimes in the words of living prophets.

Perhaps Robbie will die. One mother whom I know faced this situation in her family. The parents, the children (a "grown-up" seven-year-old, an almost-ready-for-school four-year-old, and a busy two-year-old), and the grandparents were all stunned to learn that their baby, a darling eight-month-old, had a rapidly growing brain tumor. A family council was held, prayers were offered, blessings given. The children were loved and taught and, except for the two-year-old, were helped by a professional therapist. The mother now says that she wished that little one, who they felt was too young to understand any explanation, had been included "right up front," because she had long-lasting images of her little sister "in a box" and being "put away." The baby endured surgeries and chemotherapy, pain and nausea and distress, for more than a year. Her parents and her siblings also learned much of endurance, of patience and trust, but the weeks and months were long and difficult before peace and acceptance came.

There were times of questioning, even anger, when it seemed to them as though prayers and blessings were not being heard. Even though the parents knew that they were not to blame for their baby's trial, there were occasional feelings of doubt or guilt: "If only I had rested more when I was pregnant. If only I had not drunk Diet Coke. If only. If only." It has been ten years now since the baby's death, and all of the family have come to a deeper understanding after this "trial of their faith." All are mature in their compassion for others and are strong in their testimonies. They feel it was "a pivotal growth point" in their lives, that they have learned to accept both suffering and loss and now try harder to be and to become an eternal family. They are finding joy in each other, family fun in new adventures, and appreciation for the wonder of every day. Ordinary day, help me realize what a treasure you are!

Sometimes the trial involves children even when it is not their personal challenge, just as that busy two-year-old was affected by the illness of her baby sister. One such experience came to our family when my elderly father came to live with us following a stroke. "Would it be all right if I stay here tonight? I think my family will be coming tomorrow." Although we were his only living family, this was my dad's plea almost every evening after his move to our home. The illness had not affected him much physically, but he no longer recognized any of us except my husband and our eldest daughter. To them he would say wistfully, "I wish Joy would come to see me." I'm not sure where he thought he was, nor who he thought I was, but there seemed to be no way to explain so that he could understand.

During the ensuing months he gradually became more and more dependent, needing help with eating and bathing, walking and dressing, including all the personal tasks of living. Our older children, especially, became adept at these kinds of assistance. He eventually suffered another stroke and passed quietly from this life. This was a tender time for all of us, a giving time, when we had the opportunity to care for him. Our children learned a little more of the sweetness of service and came to see the blessing as well as the sacrifice involved.

His tousled head on his mother's arm, his tear-stained face lifted, a little boy asked the question about his dog's terrible accident. His love for old Rover was deep, and parting was tender and poignant. The Lord does help us answer even such questions. He tells us of the creation of all animals (surely that includes this one, just hit by a car!), and also their resurrection.

Elder Joseph Fielding Smith had this to say: "Do animals have spirits? If so, will they obtain the resurrection, and if so, where will they go? The simple answer is that animals do have spirits, and that through the redemption made by our Savior they will come forth in the resurrection to enjoy the blessing of immortal life. . . . As to where [they] will go after the resurrection we can only express an opinion. John saw many of them in heaven in the presence of God. It is very probable that they, like mankind, will be distributed in the various kingdoms."[2] This understanding will be of at least some comfort to a little boy who stands in need of comfort.

The news given by her obstetrician to Sister Ellet can be shocking to the family, and they will have much to learn and do even as they are trying to understand its implications. A good friend, himself a pediatrician, had this experience at the birth of a precious daughter:

> How to survive? It was nearly midnight [when the baby was born]. I made three calls—one to my partner, one to my parents, one to [my wife's] parents. Within thirty minutes we had a family reunion in the hall just off the labor and delivery suite. My colleague, of course, only confirmed the diagnosis and kindly began the introduction to mental retardation and the other special problems of Down's Syndrome to the assembled relatives. I concentrated on giving support to and receiving support from [my wife]. . . .
>
> For me the moment of irrevocable attachment came a few hours later. . . . A well-meaning and much-beloved relative had shared with us the hope that she "might be taken soon" but . . . I loved this little newborn, and I no longer cared so much that she was "a Down's" as that she was "our Melinda."
>
> We told Jennifer, aged seven, first of all our children. She . . . wept, not for herself so much but because she feared the "making-fun" that others would direct at her little sister. A little later we told Meghan, aged five, who took it matter-of-factly and pledged ongoing affection for this already beloved little baby. Troy, aged two, was urged not to hug her too tightly; that was enough for his years.
>
> It is now nearly a year since that June midnight, and Melinda is

more "Mindy" than she is "Down's." She is very reinforcing and is a delight to all the family.[3]

We know that not all mental retardation is found at birth. This kind of "wind" can "beat upon [our] house" at any time as the result of disease or accident, even into old age. At whatever age loved ones are assured that mental abilities are impaired, for whatever reason, there is likely to be the same kind of grieving, the same concern for the future, the same adjustment to the reality. We can at such a time have faith that, as President Spencer W. Kimball said: "[The Lord] has promised us that he will be our tender tutor. . . . 'Be of good cheer, for I will lead you along' (D&C 78:18). He will not ask us to bear more than we can bear nor thrust upon us that for which we are not yet ready."[4] We can know, and this surely, that He will help us, guide us, and give us strength beyond our own if we but place our trust in Him and help our children to do so.

What of the wind that blows with the diagnosis of Alzheimer's disease? Even though we had suspected such a condition, it was a tender and difficult day to hear a much-respected neurologist pronounce its reality. How shall we as a family cope? What will he do now that he must no longer drive? Is his desk at the office merely a courtesy? Is Dad aware that it is? How will he feel about being released from his Church assignment? Can we still serve a mission together?

This wonderful, active, bright, caring individual was now facing what, we were told, could be two years or twenty. After tears and hugs and blessings given by our sons, and assurances that each of our children wanted to help, we remembered the promises that our Father would surely help us all, that the Savior had "descended below . . . all" (D&C 122:8) we may have ahead of us. Dave really didn't want to be a trouble or a burden to anyone. He had always appreciated the thought expressed by Jack London:

> I would rather be ashes than dust! I would rather that my spark should burn out in a brilliant blaze than it should be stifled by dry rot. I would rather be a superb meteor, every atom of me in magnificent glow, than a sleepy and permanent planet. The proper function of man is to live, not to exist. I shall not waste my days in trying to prolong them. I shall use my time.[5]

We discovered that sometimes one doesn't have the opportunity to make that choice! I look at Dave now, slumped in his big chair, leaning slightly to the left, or curled up on his bed, diapered, needing to be fed and bathed and dressed, yet still nearly always cheerful. I think back on our mission (we did have the wonderful blessing of spending eighteen months in the Tennessee Nashville Mission). He was still able to visit and bear his testimony, and what a great experience we had! I remember once wishing the wonderful young missionaries with whom we served could have known Dave when he was leading scores of Boy Scouts on fifty-mile wilderness hikes, teaching and inspiring university graduate students, helping and teaching our own children. Then I thought that maybe, just maybe, at some future time those missionaries would remember how to face with courage and dignity whatever challenges come into their lives. That might be a better lesson. It has been more than twelve years since that first diagnosis, and we have no idea how much more time we have together in mortality, but we feel generally at peace and grateful for all our blessings, including the "rain and winds and floods." Indeed, "sweet is the peace the gospel brings" (*Hymns,* no. 14) for we know that our Redeemer lives, and that the resurrection is real! "As in Adam all die, so in Christ shall all be made alive" (1 Corinthians 15:22).

Some people do not understand this, and their suffering at the time of death is surely intensified. One such person was Sam Davis, a young Civil War hero whose boyhood home we visited while we were on our mission. He had been captured and was to be put to death by the Northern army. The night before his execution he wrote this letter to his mother:

Dear Mother,

Oh how painful it is to write to you. I have got to die tomorrow morning—to be hung by the Federals. Mother, do not grieve for me. I must bid you goodbye forevermore. Mother, I do not hate to die. Give my love to all.

> Your Dear Son,
> Sam

Mother tell the children all to be good. I wish I could see all of you once more, but I never, never will no more. Mother and Father, do not forget me, think of me when I am dead, but do not grieve for me, it will not do any good.[6]

How grateful we are to know that Sam and all others who die without a knowledge of the restored gospel will yet have an opportunity to hear and respond to it!

To a child facing the death of himself or a loved one, Elder Boyd K. Packer has written a clear and sweet explanation. He compares the spirit and the body to his hand in a glove. They move together, but when he removes the glove, it can no longer move, whereas his hand can still move and work, even as can our spirits after separation from our bodies. This separation we call death. He explains to the children a bit about the premortal life and why we come to earth, the resurrection, and the Atonement in terms that a child can understand. He explains our relationship to our Father in Heaven and to the Savior and our need to be obedient to them: they love us and want us to return to them, and we can if we follow their counsel.[7]

Sometimes, we know, there are parents who have consistently tried to be good parents and to rear righteous children but whose sons or daughters have chosen another way of life. We read in the Book of Mormon of a similar experience Alma had, not with his own children but with his people: "And it came to pass that . . . he was journeying thither, being weighed down with sorrow, wading through much tribulation and anguish of soul, because of the wickedness of the people" (Alma 8:14).

Sometimes, of course, the children who stray are not wicked and do live honorable and upright lives, but are without the Church or the gospel. This, too, is a heartache for the parents, who want to have all their children together eternally. There is hope, however, for all these parents, even though the winds at times seem fierce. President Gordon B. Hinckley said at the Jordan Utah South Regional Conference, March 2, 1997, "I have here an interesting statement by Elder Orson F. Whitney: 'The Prophet Joseph Smith declared—and he never taught more comforting doctrine—that the eternal sealings of faithful parents and the divine promises made to them for valiant service in the Cause of Truth, would save not only themselves but likewise their posterity. Though some of the sheep may wander, the eye of the Shepherd is upon them, and sooner or later they will feel the tentacles of Divine Providence reaching after them and drawing them back to the fold. Either in this life or the life to come, they will return. They will have to pay their debt to justice; they will suffer for their sins; and may tread a thorny path; but if it leads them at last, like the penitent Prodigal, to a loving and forgiving father's heart and home, the painful experience will not have been in vain. Pray for your careless and disobedient children; hold on to them with your faith; hope on, trust on, till you see the salvation of God' (Conference Report, April 1929)."

President Hinckley added, "If any of you have a child or loved one in that condition, do not give up. Pray for them and love them and reach out to them and help them."8

It is true for all of us that the winds will blow and beat upon our houses. It is true, also, that our houses will stand if they are built upon the rock of Jesus Christ. Whatever adversity or difficulty we experience can be met with courage and faith, and even joy. President Spencer W. Kimball said something that has been of great comfort to me:

> We sometimes think we would like to know what lies ahead, but sober thought brings us back to accepting life a day at a time and magnifying and glorifying that day. . . .
>
> We knew before we were born that we were coming to the earth for bodies and experience and that we would have joys and sorrows, ease and pain, comforts and hardships, health and sickness, successes and disappointments, and we knew also that after a period of life we would die. We accepted all these eventualities with a glad heart, eager to accept both the favorable and unfavorable. We eagerly accepted the chance to come earthward even though it might be for only a day or a year. Perhaps we were not so much concerned whether we should die of disease, or accident, or of senility. We were willing to take life as it came and as we might organize and control it, and this without murmur, complaint, or unreasonable demands. . . .
>
> With all its troubles life offers us the tremendous privilege to grow in knowledge and wisdom, faith and works, preparing to return and share God's glory.9

And again from Alma: "And now . . . I would that ye should

remember, that as much as ye shall put your trust in God even so much ye shall be delivered out of your trials, and your troubles, and your afflictions, and ye shall be lifted up at the last day" (Alma 38:5).

NOTES

1. George Q. Cannon, *Collected Discourses,* comp. Brian H. Stuy (Burbank: B.H.S. Publishing, 1988), 2:185.

2. Joseph Fielding Smith, *Answers to Gospel Questions,* vol. 2 (Salt Lake City: Deseret book, 1958), pp. 48, 51.

3. George H. Durham II, "What If You Are the Doctor?," in *We Have Been There,* comp. Terrel Dougan, Lynn Isbell, and Patricia Vyas (Nashville: Abingdon Press, 1983), pp. 35–38.

4. Spencer W. Kimball, *The Teachings of Spencer W. Kimball,* ed. Edward L. Kimball (Salt Lake City: Bookcarft, 1982), p. 254.

5. Jack London, as found in *Richard Evans' Quote Book,* comp. Richard L. Evans (Salt Lake City: Publishers Press, 1971), p. 40.

6. From the visitor's pamphlet at the Sam Davis Home, Smyrna, Tennessee.

7. See Boyd K. Packer, *Teach Ye Diligently* (Salt Lake City: Deseret Book, 1975), pp. 230–37.

8. Gordon B. Hinckley, *Teachings of Gordon B. Hinckley* (Salt Lake City: Deseret Book, 1997), p. 54.

9. Spencer W. Kimball, *Faith Precedes the Miracle* (Salt Lake City: Deseret Book, 1977), pp. 105–6.

CHAPTER NINE

Kindness to Be Counted On

"But my kindness shall not
depart from thee."
—3 NEPHI 22:10

by
Marilyn Jeppson Choules

Feeling loving and kind gives us the ability to see another person as just as valid and important a person as we might see ourselves. Remember, "love thy neighbor as thyself."

"And I answered him, saying: Yea, it is the love of God, which sheddeth itself abroad in the hearts of the children of men; wherefore, it is the most desirable above all things. And he spake unto me, saying: Yea, and the most joyous to the soul."

1 NEPHI 11:22–23

*N*OTHING IS MORE FUNDAMENTAL TO a loving home and a happy child than kindness. The child who receives consistent, dependable kindness from a parent is surely among the most fortunate and most blessed of children. The Savior's nature is characterized by this trait; it is a basic component of the pure love of Christ. A child will best learn to be kind through having a kind mother and/or father and by being taught the nature and necessity of kindness. We as parents learn this ourselves through desire and conscious effort.

> Behold your little ones.
> And as they looked to behold, they cast their eyes towards heaven, and they saw the heavens open, and they saw angels descending out of heaven as it were in the midst of fire; and they came down and encircled those little ones about, and they were encircled about with fire; and the angels did minister unto them (3 Nephi 17:23–24).

In this modern day and "the last days," "our little ones" need to be encircled about by the "fire" of our love and be able to feel the love of God and heaven through our love and teachings.

GOD'S LOVE FOR US IS PURE AND CONSTANT

Jesus emphasized the importance of love in all His teachings and in His example. When He was asked which of the laws was the greatest, He gave to us the basic gospel principle: "Thou shalt love the Lord thy God with all thy heart, and with all thy soul, and with all thy mind.

MARILYN JEPPSON CHOULES and her husband, Albert, live in Salt Lake City, Utah. She is a family therapist and has earned four degrees at three universities, the most recent a Ph.D. in counseling psychology from Brigham Young University. Marilyn and her husband have a combined family of six living children and twenty grandchildren, of whom she enjoys painting portraits.

"This is the first and great commandment.

"And the second is like unto it, Thou shalt love thy neighbour as thyself.

"On these two commandments hang all the law and the prophets" (Matthew 22:37–40).

Why is love so important that it forms the foundation for all other laws and commandments? Feeling love does something for the soul, like nurturing, as the sun does for plants. We grow best spiritually or emotionally when we feel loved and are able to give love in return.

I love the description of the love of God given in the conversation between Nephi and the angel. Nephi had asked for confirmation and understanding of his father's dream about the iron rod and the tree of life. The angel asked Nephi if he knew the meaning of the tree his father had seen. Nephi recorded: "And I answered him, saying: Yea, it is the love of God, which sheddeth itself abroad in the hearts of the children of men; wherefore, it is the most desirable above all things. And he spake unto me, saying; yea, and the most joyous to the soul" (1 Nephi 11:22–23).

This conversation between Nephi and the angel gives us a beautiful description of the feeling of God's love: "most desirable above all other things" and "most joyous to the soul."

Why does this love feel so wonderful? It is because God's love is pure. That means His love is based on a complete understanding of us. He loves and values us completely, just as we are today. He knows our intrinsic worth. He cherishes our souls. And He says His love and kindness will be constant. "For the mountains shall depart and the hills be removed; but my kindness shall not depart from thee, neither shall the covenant of my peace be removed, saith the Lord that hath mercy on thee" (Isaiah 54:10; 3 Nephi 22:10).

God has given us examples of specific ways in which He loves us and He wants us to love each other.[1] The Savior explains: "As the Father hath loved me, so have I loved you: continue ye in my love" (John 15:9).

As we learn to understand the other person as a valid individual and to focus on his or her feelings and needs, we can learn to stretch ourselves and to love with the same sort of kindness and consistency that God does.

True Understanding and Concern Lead to Kindness

Feeling loving and kind gives us the ability to see another person as just as valid and important a person as we might see ourselves. Remember, "love thy neighbor as thyself." Doesn't this suggest putting ourselves in the "other person's shoes," allowing that his perceptions, feelings, and needs are just as important as ours? When our love is given out of true concern and acceptance of the other person and his or her needs, our behavior will always be kind and loving, we will be able *only* to be kind and loving. The consistent love and kindness our children need will be present in us and felt by them when we truly believe that "you and I are equal in value and importance." This love, born out of true valuing and of concern for another person, reminds one of the love Jonathan had for David.

Saul was king of Israel, Jonathan was his son. After David had killed Goliath, Jonathan met David. Jonathan could have been jealous because his father, Saul, esteemed David so highly, but instead we have recorded in the scriptures the beginning of one of the greatest examples of love, kindness, and loyalty.

"And it came to pass, when he had made an end of speaking unto Saul, that the soul of Jonathan was knit with the soul of David, and Jonathan loved him as his own soul.

"Then Jonathan and David made a covenant, because he loved him as his own soul.

"And Jonathan stripped himself of the robe that was upon him, and gave it to David, and his garments, even to his sword, and to his bow, and to his girdle" (1 Samuel 18:1, 3–4).

I think the phrase in verse one, "Jonathan loved him as his own soul," is significant. He was able to give David his best *because* he "loved him as his own soul."

There are times, however, when as much as we want or try to feel love and acceptance for our children, our actions don't reflect it. For most of us, our natural earthly experiences include some mistreatment, some feeling of being used or taken advantage of, or even mean and hurtful treatment. This often can put us on the defensive. We feel a need to protect ourselves, minimally to put up a wall or set a boundary. These feelings and needs come from fear. We need not fear, though, when we remember that we each can choose our own response to another's agenda for us. Jesus set a great example for us. After He had performed the miracle of the loaves and the fishes some men wanted to make Him king. He quietly removed Himself. "When Jesus therefore perceived that they would come and take him by force, to make him a king, he departed again into a mountain himself alone" (John 6:15).

We always have a choice in response to another person's behavior, a choice as to both how we feel and how we behave. There are times when we realize that the choices we are making may be hurtful to our children. When this is the case we need to take the responsibility to seek additional help for ourselves.

WE LEARN TO LOVE AND ACCEPT OUR CHILDREN IN THE SAME WAY WE LOVE AND ACCEPT GOD

Learning to feel and give love consistently as Jesus and God are able to is an ongoing process. The activities that will help us more consistently to love our children are the same as the familiar activities we use to learn to love God and feel His love. These activities are prayer or communication, study, and service.

Prayer or Communication

A relationship requires communication. Communication is meant to be a two-way process. This means equal time spent talking and listening. We speak to share our own perspective, our own feelings, and our own needs. We listen to understand the perspective, the feelings, and the needs of the other. Let us look at how this basic process can work in our relationship with our children.

As parents we usually give direction to motivate our child to do the actions we have decided it is best for him or her to do. "Make your bed before breakfast." "Don't yell at your brother." "Get your homework done." "You've got to be ready to go in two minutes." "No, you can't go to that party this Friday. It's our family campout." All of this is speaking in one direction, parent to child. There is bound to be some of this during our years of parenting. Children have individual spirits, however. They have individual perspectives and needs. Without some patterns of listening within the family, a child may begin to feel angry and rebellious.

Consider this example: A young mother with five small children was busy at the kitchen counter fixing dinner. Her young son Tommy came running in and said, "Mom, Mom." "Yes," she responded, as she continued working at the counter. "Mom," he implored, "listen to me." "I'm listening," she replied as she continued working. "No," Tommy said, "Listen with your face!" In his young four-year-old mind, he knew he needed her full attention, face to face. "Listen with your face!"

Listening requires giving full attention. It isn't just the content of what the child is saying that he or she needs us to hear, but also to understand what is being felt, what is needed. This we can only learn as we listen to understand. We do this by asking tentative questions about the feelings and perceptions of the speaking child. Listen to a conversation between Ann and her mother.

Ann: "Can you believe that teacher? She yelled at me just because I picked up my pencil during music hour. I was just moving it out of the way."

Mom: "It sounds like you feel pretty mad at Mrs. Jones."

Ann: "Yes, and she didn't understand I was just moving it."

Mom: "Kind of misunderstood too."

Ann: "Yes, I wonder why she was so angry over such a little thing."

Mom: "You mean, perhaps she had other worries which may have triggered her sharpness with you."

Ann: "Yes, she's never treated me like that before. I hope she's okay. I should have obeyed the rule."

Mom's listening to understand Ann's feeling enabled Ann to examine her feelings and resolve her own anger. She was then able to ponder her teacher's perceptions and feelings. It would have been easy for Mom to dismiss Ann's first angry remark with a response like, "Now, Ann, you need to obey the teacher's rules, and if you were wrong you shouldn't feel angry at her." This would probably have shut Ann down and she would have lost the opportunity to be listened to and understood by Mom. She very probably would have stayed focused on the wrongness of the teacher's anger and may not have been able to come to the point of taking responsibility for her own small mistake. This listening to understand acknowledges to our child that his or her feelings and needs are just as important as our own.

Study

A relationship improves as we learn different approaches to the problems we face. The responses that seem most natural to us are the ones we have seen taken by people around us. These might not always be the most effective. We need to look for new responses. We can seek and use all available resources and opportunities to learn the very best parenting skills. Resources can be:

— Individual prayer for guidance

— Scriptural direction and support

— Recommended and documented parenting books

— Competent counseling (professional as well as suggestions from seasoned, mature adults)

— Specialty resources for such conditions as attention deficit disorder, obsessive compulsive disorder, conduct disorder.

We have never been parents before this life. We can't automatically expect to know all the answers or best ways to work with and help our children. We are lucky to have so many resources available to help us with the complicated issues of our day.

Service

As we invest ourselves in anything (person, activity, or thing) we care more about the outcome. It is a natural process. The giving of ourselves enhances our valuing of that which we serve.

My mother gave me excellent advice after the birth of our first child when she encouraged me to share the night feedings with my husband. "We love those whom we serve," she said. As I've pondered that counsel during the different stages of my life, I know it is true. Likewise a child who is only served becomes self-centered. He can't begin to see his parents as individuals with feelings and needs of their own. He will only see them as vehicles to satisfy his needs and desires.

Some years ago I learned that one of my sisters I visited as a visiting teacher needed to stay in bed for the remaining five months of her sixth pregnancy. My partner and I organized and made sure the family had meals brought in for several days. Then I received a call from her husband. He said: "We appreciate the wonderful meals we have been enjoying. Our children have felt the love and kindness of the ward family. We are so grateful. However, I need to have you stop. My wife has sacrificed and served our family. This is a great opportunity for me to help our children learn to serve her. They will appreciate her much more as they learn to do for her many of the tasks she has done for them."

I have since moved from that ward, but recently I saw that mother at a mall with her oldest daughter, who was pushing her own oldest child in a stroller. They were laughing and chatting together. What a picture of mutual love and kindness!

This ongoing process of prayer, study, and service is an interweaving, interconnected pattern. When our relationships are built upon understanding, we become more motivated to serve one another. We have a responsibility to increase our understanding of our individual children in every possible way.

We Can Treat Difficult Behaviors with Kindness

It is easy to be kind when our children are behaving, but sometimes our best efforts don't produce the results we are hoping for. At moments like this, kindness may seem like lenience, but *we can be kindly firm*. For the purpose of this chapter, I will discuss a few types of children's difficult behaviors. I hope the examples presented here will trigger new ideas for dealing with similar behaviors readers may be coping with.

Dealing with Disobedience

Disobedience is failing to follow the rule or direction given. It may be manifest in stubbornness, rebellion, ignoring, disregarding, mischievousness, obstinacy, or waywardness. For example: The family rule is to put toys away before bedtime at eight o'clock. The child continues to play rather than put toys away when reminded at 7:45 P.M.

We can find guidance in the scriptures and in latter-day leaders. "A soft answer turneth away wrath" (Proverbs 15:1).

> No power or influence can or ought to be maintained by virtue of the priesthood, only by persuasion, by long-suffering, by gentleness and meekness and by love unfeigned.
>
> Reproving betimes with sharpness, when moved upon by the Holy Ghost; and then showing forth afterwards an increase of love toward him whom thou hast reproved, lest he esteem him to be his enemy (D&C 121:41, 43).

> Discipline with love. "Discipline" and "punishment" are not synonymous. Punishment suggests hurting, paying someone back for a wrong committed. Discipline implies an action directed toward a goal . . . of helping the recipient to improve himself (William E. Homan as quoted by Elder Ben Banks).[2]

> Discipline is organized love, and children develop properly in an atmosphere of love, with adequate guidelines to shape their lives and habits. More children are punished for mimicking their parents than ever for disobeying them. We should *be* what we want to *see* (Elder LeGrand R. Curtis).[3]

Psychologist Lynn Scoresby tells the following story:

All people need to be able to "take a stand" with their peers. A sixteen-year-old son of mine was having trouble in this area. His friends were allowed to stay out until one o'clock on Friday and Saturday nights. I felt it was important for him to be home by midnight on Saturday night. I explained the reasons for the rule. I was waiting for him that following Saturday evening. He arrived just before one o'clock. His explanation,"Well, they were driving and didn't want to leave early." "You can call me," I said, "or get them to come earlier, but you still need to be home by midnight. You'll need to try it again next Saturday night." You mean you're not going to ground me?" he asked. "You have to go out to be able to practice coming home on time; now let's go have a bowl of ice cream," I said. It took several Saturday nights before he came home on time. But he gained the ability to take a stand with his peers and we had a lot of ice cream and fun late night conversation.[4]

The chances are that this son felt very loved as he was learning to obey the rule. First, he was important enough to Dad to be waited up for. Second, Dad didn't get angry when his son didn't make it home on time. And third, he discussed options for being successful next time. Then he wanted to hear about his son's evening over a bowl of ice cream. What a great example! No anger, no vengeance, no criticism. Just loving, concerned, interested, and fun help.

It's easy to feel frustrated and critical when a child continues to disobey. We feel a responsibility for our children's behavior, so we may feel inconvenienced, disappointed, or embarrassed when their behavior is disobedient or inappropriate. We need to remember that (1) learning takes practice and (2) the rule often fits an adult agenda more than a child's desire. Learning in this world, especially in this time of confusing messages, is not an easy or fast task. Personalities of children are different. The ease or speed with which one child learns may be very different from that of another, even among our own children.

Acting Out

Willful, disruptive, or destructive behavior, including hurting others, yelling, name calling, breaking things, or deliberately creating a mess, are forms of acting out.

Usually the need to act out is fed by a need for attention, validation, clearer understanding of what's going on, or a strong sense of "I'm okay." If we only give consequences for the behavior, we may control or curb it, but the feelings and needs of the child will still exist. The bulk of what the child needs is to feel loved and valuable.

As a therapist I witnessed a conversation between an adolescent son and his father. "Why do you do these things you know are wrong? You know it makes me so angry when you hit your sister and swear at your mom," said Dad. The son answered, "You're always so busy, but at least when you hit me, I know you notice me." What a revelation! Dad is trying to be a good dad by getting him to stop hurting his sister or swearing at Mom. But what his son needs is loving time and attention. Children work hard to get their needs met, one way or the other. And they need loving time, which gives them a clear message that they are valuable enough for a busy parent to give them one-on-one time. The father might put an arm around his son's shoulders with a message: "Son, let's talk about what's going on here. How shall we fix this?" Perhaps this would be the first step in a parent's responding to a child's acting out.

Terry Warner, in his *Bonds of Anguish, Bonds of Love,* tells a story about a teenage mother who really wasn't emotionally ready for parenthood. She was trying to break her pattern of lashing out at her eighteen-month-old son when he did something that annoyed her. She reported her progress to her therapist:

> I was determined not to get angry, but the next day I got angry at everything. I was tying Andrew's shoes, and as I would tie one and go to the next, he would untie it. When I would go to tie it again, he would untie the other one. When I got them both tied, he untied them with both hands at once. I was so mad I caught myself about to hit him. Then I remembered the homework and tried to think of what was right that I should do. I couldn't think of anything. As I sat there concentrating, I called Andrew over to me and put him on my lap and just sat there rocking with my arms around him and my eyes closed, trying to think of what was right. After a long time I knew the right thing was just to love him, and I started to cry and couldn't stop. I sat there hugging him.[5]

This young mother made a choice not to act on her anger but to take time out to think. As she was able to think about what was best for her son, she saw him as an individual. That's when she got in touch with her love for him and instinctively did the best thing for him.

CHILDREN LEARN TO LOVE IN THE
ENVIRONMENT OF THEIR PARENTS' LOVE

The greatest security we give our children is the love we parents demonstrate for each other and for each of them individually. When children feel the joy, peace, and power that fills the environment from this kind of parental relationship, they learn (even without realizing they are learning) to love automatically. They have experienced the feeling and they have seen the behavior. It feels natural as well as wonderful and "most joyous to the soul."

We can show our children through our example, then, in the same way God and Jesus have shown us through theirs. "As the Father hath loved me, so have I loved you: continue ye in my love" (John 15:9).

We are fortunate to have the fulness of the gospel in these latter days to help us understand the magnitude of our blessing and opportunity as parents. We will undoubtedly make mistakes. However, when we are able to feel and demonstrate our love to our children, they will be empowered to grow in the light of our love and better feel the love of our Heavenly Father and Jesus for them.

NOTES

1. The scriptures are replete with descriptions of loving and kind behavior: charity, valuing, respect, caring, concern, humility, meekness, understanding, hope, faith, peace, joy, compassion, reverence, honor, and forgiving. Some focus a little more on loving behavior: kindness, gentleness, sacrificing, serving, mercy, long-suffering, consistency, honesty, sharing, trustworthy, and patience. Romans 12:10; Galatians 5:22; Jude 1:2; Moroni 8:26; D&C 88:126; 2 Samuel 2:6; Isaiah 54:8, 10; Colossians 3:12; Matthew 5:7; John 5:10–11; John 13:1, 13–17; 1 John 3:10; Ether 12:33–34; D&C 121:41–42; Colossians 2:2.

2. William E. Homan, "How to Be a Better Parent," *Reader's Digest,* October 1969, pp. 187–91, as quoted by Ben Banks, *Ensign,* November 1993, p. 29.

3. LeGrand R. Curtis, "Happiness Is Homemade," *Ensign,* November 1990, p. 12.

4. Lynn Scoresby from classroom lecture notes in author's possession.

5. Terry Warner, *Bonds of Anguish, Bonds of Love* (Salt Lake City: The Arbinger Company, 1995), p. 9:8. Unfinished draft.

CHAPTER TEN

Nurturing Happiness

"Then shall they break
forth into joy."
—3 NEPHI 20:34

by
Jeanne Bryan Inouye

*We sometimes characterize pleasure as ephemeral and merely
sensational, and joy as lasting and truly uplifting. But among
little children—and among all who are pure and childlike—
that which brings pleasure is a source of genuine happiness.*

"Happiness is the object and design of our existence."

JOSEPH SMITH

*I*N 2 NEPHI WE LEARN THAT GOD PLACED us here on earth that we might have joy (see 2 Nephi 2:25), a teaching reiterated in the later words of the Prophet Joseph Smith that "Happiness is the object and design of our existence."[1] Pondering this concept, we sometimes characterize pleasure as ephemeral and merely sensational, and joy as lasting and truly uplifting.

But among little children—and among all who are pure and childlike—that which brings pleasure is a source of genuine happiness. The delights of childhood are good. They are a first taste of the deeper joys of Christ's gospel, to be fostered and remembered. Thus an important aspect of nurturing children is helping them to feel joy and to choose the ways of happiness. The wise steward will select and create occasions for healthy fun and guide the child in an expanding experience and understanding of joy.

We do not lack for suggestions about possibilities that are "virtuous, lovely, of good report, or praiseworthy" (Articles of Faith 1:13). Church publications, parenting magazines, and bookstore shelves are replete with ideas. If, in fact, a priesthood or Relief Society teacher asks for a list of memorable activities that enrich the lives of children, suggestions ranging from camping to service projects will soon cover the blackboard. And just ask a Sunbeam class to describe favorite activities. Such lists invariably cluster around ways to utilize holidays and holy days, to cherish our tradition and heritage, and to build relationships within our families and with others.

Indeed, we do not lack for general answers, but what each of us needs is a sustained, personal focus. We need direction as we gener-

JEANNE BRYAN INOUYE and her husband, Dillon, live in Provo, Utah, with their children, Emily and Daniel. Jeanne holds a law degree from the J. Reuben Clark Law School at Brigham Young University. She has served on the Relief Society General Board and chaired the planning committee for several BYU Women's Conferences. She is currently the ward Relief Society president.

ate, consider, and select among myriad possibilities. We might find such focus in asking three questions of our occasional, daily, and weekly activities: (1) Will this provide delight? (2) Will this promote unity? (3) Will this help us grow in Christ's example of love? Any contrived or formulaic calculation of these emphases is probably not helpful. What we all need to develop is a sensitivity to the continuum between delight and joy. If we are to be supple and balanced stewards, helping our children appreciate the small and large joys for which we have been created, we need vision, whether that means focus, depth, or peripheral glimmerings. Perhaps the following anecdotes, both personal and more general, will provide examples of the continuum between delight and joy in our varied responses to holidays, tradition and heritage, and familial relationships, immediate and extended.

HOLIDAYS AND HOLY DAYS

Most of us have holiday traditions. Regular repetition of special activities at Thanksgiving, Christmas, Hanukkah, or Chinese New Year gives the traditions extra meaning and delight. They become "markers" of the family. My own family members know that "the cousins' Christmas orchestra" is something we do and that we spend the last week of summer at Emerald Lake. And each time we repeat these activities, we remember the orchestra or the lake in past years and the loved ones who giggled together over squeaky notes and rejoiced in "the strains of redeeming love," who chuckled with us at the pluck of a pert chipmunk and gloried in God's creation of the starry mountain skies.

A phrase like "the Fourth of July" connotes for many Americans "fun" images of firecrackers, watermelon, and parades. It can also connote images of unity, as it does in the small central Utah community where my husband's parents live. Families there enjoy typical Independence Day activities—pancake breakfast in the park, fishing booths for little children, and cotton candy. All good fun. Family and community members unite as grown children travel home, bringing grandchildren to enjoy the activities with their extended families and longtime friends. Older children sometimes join cousins in the post-festivities cleanup or help grandparents return chairs or count the money generated for community projects. Sometimes conversations turn to the sacrifices of immigrant forebears who established the family in this country. Some attend patriotic services or read passages from the Declaration of Independence, remembering the Christlike love of those who risked and gave their lives to establish freedom for themselves and their posterity. The range of possible activities is wide.

All these emphases are good. Some occur with little effort, and others must be planned. Some will provide pure delight; others stretch the child and strengthen the family. The development and the needs of the children should influence the choice and creation of activities. The one superior to the other is the one that the individual and the family need at a given time. If we remain sensitive to the need for personal perspective, we are moving toward the joy that attends vision.

Holidays—originally holy days—often began, and sometimes continue, as religious observances. Among the holiest of days, the one commanded and set apart by the Lord, is the Sabbath. Partaking of the sacrament and attending Sunday meetings together is usually the core of Sunday activities. But we often have more discretionary time on Sundays than on most other days of the week. Many try to keep this a family day. In the varied approaches reflective of the need for delight, unity, and Christlike love, aware families find many pleasant and enjoyable ways to keep the Sabbath. One family's children cooked together on Sundays. Their mother prepared meals the rest of the week, but the children gave her a break on Sundays. They laughed, visited, and enjoyed one another's company as together they learned skills they would take into their adult lives.

In another family parents read to their children Sunday afternoons from the time they were young through their high school years. When they were small, the children found delight in sitting close and listening to stories. As they grew more independent, they came with scrapbooks and crafts, listening together while working on projects. Later they entered more into the discussion of the literary themes and the authors' perspectives on what brings joy and sorrow. Modifying the activity to meet the needs of maturing children, the parents kept this Sunday tradition alive and enjoyable. The desire to keep the Sabbath should remain constant; the mode varied according to need.

HERITAGE

When we think about possible activities that range from the delight of simple fun to moments of total joy, we realize how interconnected are holidays, culture, community, and family. Heritage is an abstraction that refuses definition in a vacuum. I, for example, cannot separate my heritage as part of Tooele, Utah, from family experience. In our then small town, the community maintained the city cemetery. Several weeks before Memorial Day, my own father took one or more of us children with him to begin cleaning up the family cemetery plots. Then early on Memorial Day morning we went to Grandma Bryan's house. She filled big aluminum washtubs with the lilacs, irises, peonies, or roses in season and wrapped fruit jars and coffee cans with tinfoil. We carried these to the cemetery, where we began our yearly search for the twenty or so graves that she always decorated. Many were for relatives I heard about mostly on Memorial Day.

We traveled to several cemeteries with my maternal grandmother and often stopped to visit relatives who lived nearby. I saw the two huge old trees near the graves of great-great-grandparents and learned how my great-grandmother carried water to them a bucket at a time to beautify the burial site. I still associate Memorial Day with the pleasure of cool mornings in Grandma's yard and warm afternoons in family gatherings and with the fun of cutting flowers and choosing among dripper pan cakes. But now I realize the sacredness and joy of listening to stories of progenitors and feeling the ties that bind me to people that my people loved. So on or near each Memorial Day I take my children home to the towns where our forebears lived and the plots where they are buried, and I tell them the stories I learned as a girl.

All cultures remember heritage, and their varied celebrations can be mutually instructive. With my marriage I joined my husband's Japanese-American family for their memorial activities. Their visits to gravesites always include a family prayer and expression of gratitude

for the blessings experienced because of the good lives of earlier generations. Many of the Buddhist relatives hold memorial services for
family members at certain anniversaries of the death, and the Latter-
day Saint members join with them to share stories about those who
are departed.

Like so many families exploring heritage, we've traveled to the
birthplaces of our families. Our children's grandfather came to America to meet his family's obligation as cosigners on a note secured by
their farm. When we visited Japan, his nephew took us to the mountain site where he made that decision. We visited Buddhist temples
holding genealogy records and cemeteries where inscriptions provided further data. Interwoven between the sacred moments that
bound us more closely with ancestors was the fun of quickly board-
ing the bullet train, sampling curry rice and gyoza, and puzzling out
locations written in Japanese characters.

Heritage is something we all have, but we must all work if we
want to perceive the constantly changing continuum between fun
and play inherent in our cultural and ethnic backgrounds. Some of
us may never have had a grandparent who shared memories. If not,
the memory-building begins with us. Like so many who have been
influenced by the spirit of Elijah, both Church members and non-
members, we can trace our individual heritage and consider the ways
it may have shaped our values and perceptions. If we live in the
United States we are imbued with an appreciation of many varied
backgrounds. If we are from a country peopled by one group, we may
more easily see the similarities between us and others in the group.
In all instances heritage is touchstone to identity, and exploring that
identity may highlight the fun of throwing water-filled balloons during a Thai holiday, the delight of making and sharing tamales at
Christmas, or the joy of gathering to watch the moon at its fullest in
the year because it recalls the family circle.

Again, one aspect or approach to heritage is neither qualitatively
nor quantitatively superior to the others. What matters is that we
remain sensitive to possibility and open to what is best in our particular circumstances at a given time, to what is—both in the short- and
the long-term—most conducive to the joy for which we have been
created.

FAMILY AND OTHER HUMAN RELATIONSHIPS

Among the greatest sources of joy are those that come from our association with others during mortality. Most of us feel joy with parents and siblings in loving families. But we are all part of the larger human family. Just as loving parents provide opportunities for the joy that comes from working and playing together in their home, so will they plan activities with extended family and others. As children work and play with adults, they will learn to have fun with others, to sense the commonalities in varied personalities and perspectives, and to love and serve as Christ did.

We all know stories of work and play and the ways that work becomes play. This "hindsight" may provide insight about future use of our time. Shortly after my marriage I joined my husband and his siblings to help Grandpa in the yearly potato harvest. That October the grown children, all busy in their own right, drove home to play a small, perhaps symbolic, part in the work that had sustained and built the family. Some of us sorted potatoes as they rolled past on a conveyor belt atop the combine. As the day wore on, my hands cramped from the repeated motions of picking up potatoes and dirt clods, and I looked hopefully at the sky for nightfall. But no one stopped or complained. They had spent many seasons on the combine where no one could be heard unless the equipment broke down. And they knew they could toss a few potatoes at each other, laugh together, and make the fun they remember now.

Work-fun, engendering togetherness and accomplishment, may seem harder to provide in urban environments. But we try. We've all heard someone say, "Now you know why the Creator made grass— so children will have work in the summer." Mowing and edging allow parents to teach children the delight in rendering order from disorder. Growboxes, if not gardens, provide principle and pleasure. Similarly, teaching a young adult to cook evening meals is occasionally frustrating, often fun, and usually joyful, the joy emerging from shared purpose and shared sense of accomplishment. And while the goal is usually to help the children learn to carry out these activities on their own, time spent *together* planting tomatoes or painting the fence grows sweeter in memory.

Like working together, playing together enhances family closeness. Playing can be an important way to express love and pleasure
in one another's company. How often grandparents say that if they
had the opportunity to raise their children again, they would play
more with them! And sometimes absence reinforces the value of play.
A friend, a busy young mother and widow, shared one of her children's concerns after her husband's untimely death. He had organized
the camping, hiking, and bicycling in the family, and this child wondered, "Will we ever play again?"

Through their delight in running about, in pretending, and making and playing games, children often unwittingly instruct adults
about the value of play. Playing pitcher and outfield to primary
schoolchildren in a game of kick ball may take grown-ups away from
important projects and may wear us out, but the excitement and
squeals of delight at kicking the ball and circling the bases can renew,
even as they build the family. Family basketball, board games or jig-
saw puzzles, tennis with Mom or a dinner date with Dad—the possibilities are too varied to list.

Each of us has opportunities to help our children enjoy and
rejoice in family, but they vary according to circumstance. A friend
told me of a member of her Relief Society, a Filipino sister forced to
seek employment in another Asian country to provide basic necessi-
ties for her children. Leaving them in the care of loved ones, she
relied on constant letters, then cassette tapes and telephone calls, and
always on prayer, to share her love and help her children develop a
sense of family. Their activities, among them writing to Mother and
attending church in her absence, helped bond them together and
instill in them the joy of gospel living. In these challenging circumstances, this mother looked for and found ways to teach and share
happiness because she focused on finding ways to help her children
experience pleasure, unity, and joy in family interaction.

Our appreciation for the meaning of family is expanded as we
have fun with extended family members. Overnights with cousins,
campouts with relatives, and family dinners teach the pleasure and
joy of our larger family and prepare us to reach out to others—to all
of God's children, who are also our family.

Extended family celebrations of happy occasions can be fun for everyone. Think of a family wedding or a missionary homecoming or a birthday party. Many of us have images of charmed little girls gathered around a beautiful bride, or younger sisters and brothers tiptoeing for a first glance of their missionary disembarking from a plane. Often these occasions are celebrations of union and reunion here on earth that turn our thoughts to union and reunion in eternity. Even our sad occasions have their joy. Funerals and the attendant family gatherings are filled with memories of fun times together, kindnesses, and love. Often they are celebrations of good and unselfish lives, testimonials of God's plan and his love, and times of renewal and recommitment by surviving loved ones. Parents' thoughtful consideration of appropriate activities for children, whether bundling small packets of bird seed to shower the departing bride and groom or singing with a grandchildren's chorus at a funeral, can nurture joy. And at these special times our sure and tender testimonies of the joy promised those exalted in an eternal unit can strengthen our children.

The concept of family easily enlarges for those actively involved in a church. Latter-day Saint ward activities, for example, provide a natural opportunity for children to work and play beyond the experience provided by the immediate and extended family. Youth groups may clear a forest trail or children prepare breakfast for the bishopric. The Primary may fly kites on a spring morning, Scouts may dig for ancient fish in a fossil quarry, young women may share the intricacies of computer research in family history centers. Parents and children, single Church members, and older couples get to know one another, and like one another, as they practice for the ward melodrama or clean a yard or paint a house. To experience fun, delight, and joy in the group exchange of a ward setting is a step toward expanding our understanding of kinship with all.

That kinship extends naturally from the ward family to "saints" outside the ward or stake and, as our hearts are "knit together in love," to Church members everywhere. For many years a family friend joined us for dinner and home evening on Monday evenings. She was an elderly woman living alone, retired but still a teacher. Our children grew up with her visits, looking forward to our drives to and from her home, talk around the table, and the treats she always brought for dessert. With age and incapacity she could no longer live at home, and we spent our home evenings with her in the care center where she lived. Now the children brought the treats—cookies made from the good recipes she had passed on. She loved our children, and they learned to love her.

Even as children build relationships in immediate, extended, and church families, most make friends in their schools and wider communities. As children begin to extend themselves in these broader circles, parents who model adult friendships can help them discover that it's fun for people of all ages, backgrounds, and cultures to be together and learn from one another. Wise parents can begin early to teach an appreciation of others whose backgrounds and culture may differ from ours. Reading about children in other lands, learning a few words in several languages, and visiting local ethnic festivals are some of the many "eye" and "door openers." We can invite over newly returned missionaries to tell our families about the people they have learned to love. We can encourage our daughter to make friends with her new classmate from Spain and our son to get to know his Thai coach as well as play soccer. We can widen our own circle of friends to include good people of many backgrounds—Church members and not, similarly educated and not, married and not. And we can include our children in these friendships.

True, we can invite over the new family in the ward, but we can also invite Dad's students or new acquaintances. Children can help set the table, prepare, or serve the meal. Most important, they share the opportunity to host the guests, welcoming them into the home, and participating in conversation around the table. They learn how adults converse and socialize with others. Attention spans may be short when children are young, and they may ask to be excused shortly after dinner. But as they grow, they learn that it is fun to get to know David's dad next door or the amateur astronomer who wants to show the Andromeda Galaxy to anyone who's interested. When Dad's Peruvian student brings his family to dinner, the children may learn that their school experiences differ significantly. At the same time they may learn that language differences need not be barriers to fun on the backyard trampoline.

And what else can we do? We can look to the Lord "in every

thought" (D&C 6:36), prayerfully contemplating the needs of our children and the ways we may bless them. Perhaps, as did families in one African branch, we frugally save generator fuel so that our families may spend Christmas Day watching videotapes of conference and rejoicing in the opportunity to hear God's prophets. Perhaps we spend an afternoon looking for Civil War bullets or following the ruts on a pioneer trail or studying the mortarless stone walls of high Peru, and talk about our heritage. We may clean offices together in the early morning to pay rent or keep a family member in the mission field, or we may gather to sing or dance to folk songs. As we seek God's guidance, He will help us make appropriate choices that will bring delight and happiness.

We are all children of God, and we rejoice in our awareness that the words spoken in 2 Nephi were addressed to a group of people who may not have looked much like us or experienced the ethnic and cultural awarenesses to which we have been born. What reassurance to know that the words of the Savior that point us to family, heritage, and unity transcend the transient markers of culture and country! They are true, and they speak to the eternal identities we have in common. As children, we are to have joy. As we read and reread the words of Christ and prayerfully ask how we are to apply them in our lives, we will be directed to thoughts and activities that will magnify our individual circumstances and callings.

These callings will be what they have always been, the beginning and the end, to teach children that they may have joy, that they might experience abundant delight during childhood and that they might be prepared for the greater joys of the gospel of Christ, the joys of unity and harmony in family, of sharing and learning together in their wards and communities, and of becoming like Christ, who knows us and loves us and takes pleasure in our growth and who has commanded us to love one another.

To take joy in our mortal existence, in the use of our bodies, in the beauty of God's creations, in the privilege to associate with and lift one another, in our own eventual redemption through Christ, and in the redemption of every soul who will come unto him: this is the "object and design of our existence."

NOTES

1. Joseph Smith, *Teachings of the Prophet Joseph Smith,* comp. Joseph Fielding Smith (Salt Lake City: Deseret Book, 1959), p. 255.

CHAPTER ELEVEN

Beautiful Music: Melodies of the Heart

"With the voice together
they shall sing."
—3 NEPHI 20:32

by
Barbara N. Richards

Great music was an integral part of my family's home life, and even while I was a tiny infant my mother would put me in a wicker clothes basket, gather her mending and darning, and take me to the morning rehearsals of the Los Angeles Philharmonic Orchestra at the Hollywood Bowl.

"Music has boundless powers for moving families toward greater spirituality and devotion to the gospel. Latter-day Saints should fill their homes with the sound of worthy music."

FIRST PRESIDENCY

*W*OULDN'T IT BE FASCINATING TO KNOW what music was sung and played in our premortal life? It would have to be "heavenly" music, don't you think? Even though the veil of forgetfulness is drawn over us when we enter this earth life, the power of music seems to remain with us.

Let me tell you about a young mother in my former stake. She was expecting her sixth baby and would become overwhelmed and frazzled from time to time. In the evening she would routinely take time to relax by listening to a recording of the Pachelbel Canon, a calm, soothing piece of music. Then, after the baby was born, when he became fussy and colicky a few minutes of the Pachelbel Canon would relax and lull him until he fell peacefully asleep.

My own experience with music also began before I was born. Great music was an integral part of my family's home life, and even while I was a tiny infant my mother would put me in a wicker clothes basket, gather her mending and darning, and take me to the morning rehearsals of the Los Angeles Philharmonic Orchestra at the Hollywood Bowl.

Since I was the youngest of six children, my ears were quickly attuned to musical masterpieces because we listened to them on the radio, we had a Victrola with thick heavy records of Caruso and other artists, and we often had musical evenings in our home where artist friends and family would perform. It was always a thrill for me to be allowed to stay up late and listen when my parents had their "musical soirees." In addition, each of us children learned to play the piano or another instrument—or else!

BARBARA N. RICHARDS *served as the keynote speaker at the 1984 Church Music Workshop and has developed a hymn directing course and a music appreciation series for young children entitled "Discover Music." Barbara and her husband, Lynn, recently moved to Utah from their long-established home in Long Beach, California. They are the parents of six children.*

Wintertime meant concerts at the Philharmonic in downtown L.A. with famous artists. Summertime meant the Hollywood Bowl, and in those years only the best classical world-renowned musicians performed. My mother would pack a picnic lunch for my brother and me because we always arrived at the Bowl around 3:00 P.M. for the 8:30 P.M. concert. Coming early we could get front row seats for 25 and 50 cents just above the expensive boxes. As mother chatted with other early birds, my brother and I would be free to run over the hills and watch as the stage was set up. The Bowl personnel knew us so well that they invited us one year to assist with the production of *Madam Butterfly*. A group of us sat at shady picnic tables making pale pink paper cherry blossoms for several days. Of course, the opera had our undivided attention when it was performed. We also learned concert etiquette as we sat listening to great music. By being surrounded by great music very early, I learned to love it very early.

What are the three main parts of us? The intelligence (or mind); the spirit (the literal spirit child of heavenly parents); and the body, this made of tangible material (created by earthly parents). Let us consider how music affects these three parts.

Beginning with the mind, what are your thoughts as you listen to various kinds of music, and what might be the thoughts of your child? Music can be happy, contemplative, spiritual, reflective, sad, comforting, restorative, uplifting, and can stir our emotions. Music can also be saturated with evil thought and thus be a corruptive influence. Used like this it is a subtle but powerful way for Satan to lead away our children "carefully down to hell" (2 Nephi 28:21).

Once I made an exercise of marking in my new set of scriptures every reference to music, singing, and instruments. A pattern emerged that gave me insight into the spirit and use of music. Here are a few examples: *Psalm 9:2* "I will sing praise to thy name, O thou most High." *Ephesians 5:19* "Speaking to yourselves in psalms and hymns and spiritual songs, singing and making melody in your heart to the Lord." *Alma 36:22* "Yea, methought I saw . . . God sitting upon his throne, surrounded with numberless concourses of angels, in the attitude of singing and praising their God; yea, and my soul did long to be there." *Moses 7:53* "Blessed are they of whom I have spoken, for they shall come forth with songs of everlasting joy." *D&C 25:12* "For my soul delighteth in the song of the heart; yea, the song of the righteous is a prayer unto me, and it shall be answered with a blessing upon their heads."

In our Bible Dictionary there are dozens of references to songs, singing, and hymns, and the pattern, I found, is *praise* and *joy!* Let our minds, therefore, be filled with *praise* and *joy!*

Our mind and spirit blend together as music moves us. Some years ago Elder Boyd K. Packer warned us: "In our day, music itself has been corrupted. Music can, by its tempo, by its beat, by its intensity, *dull the spiritual sensitivity of men.*"[1]

In the Pearl of Great Price we learn that God "created all things . . . spiritually before they were naturally upon the face of the earth" (Moses 3:5). Even plants. Extensive experiments in controlled conditions have shown that various plants respond either negatively, passively, or positively to a variety of music. Those grown along with calm, devotional music grew profusely. They developed deep roots and many blossoms, and actually leaned toward the sound. Conversely, plants exposed continuously to the loud, pounding acid rock sound withered and died.[2] Might our children's spirits feel similar responses—either withering or blossoming?

This reminds us of another scripture from the Book of Mormon, which Nephi's brothers, the sons of Ishmael, and their wives forgot the Lord on their long voyage to the promised land, "they began to dance, and to sing, and to speak with much rudeness . . . yea, they were lifted up unto exceeding rudeness" (1 Nephi 18:9). One has only to drive the streets in any urban area today to experience blasting stereos and "exceeding rudeness."

An inspiring example of music touching the spirit comes from the story of a severely autistic eleven-year-old boy. Experts had given up on him, but his mother noticed that he reacted to music, and she enrolled him in the Center for Music Therapy. He responded very little at first. The therapists were pessimistic, but during the seventeenth session the breakthrough happened. "As his therapist paused in his playing of 'Swanee River,' Joshua began to play, repeating the entire song note for note. His face radiated pure joy. Music gives Joshua an essential sense of mastery in a world from which he would otherwise be almost entirely withdrawn."[3]

Now, how does our physical body respond to music? Scientists report that music has an influence on all the functions of our body. Musical sounds can make us tense or relaxed. Rhythms can affect the heart, body muscles, and motor nerves. Certain kinds of music can actually weaken us, but good music and nature sounds can be strengthening. After researching for twenty-five years, John Diamond, M.D., discovered that "our bodies can discriminate between beneficial and detrimental sounds" and that "our bodies have a pulse, and so does music." He further states that "surrounded by the right sounds, we all can be invigorated, energized, and balanced."[4]

As parents we take great care in providing the best possible food for our children. We know their health and growth depends on the most nutritious food we can provide, and we hope that as they grow up they will continue eating good wholesome meals, seldom resorting to "junk" food. It is the same with "junk" music. Let us offer our children a variety of good, healthy music to nourish their bodies as well as their minds and spirits. Our children, and their children, must be given every opportunity to be raised with every aspect of their lives in tune with the Spirit.

It is possible to live our whole life without seeing a Rembrandt or a Gainsborough, without reading Shakespeare or Dickens, without listening to Mozart or Brahms. But then we would be missing some of the greatest treasures our Heavenly Father has placed on earth to help uplift and enrich our lives. For a woman to bring culture and refinement to her home is a responsibility and a joy. "If there is anything virtuous, lovely, or of good report, or praiseworthy, we seek after these things" (Articles of Faith 1:13).

While music fads come and go, the "classics" remain year after year, century after century. Why? Because frequently the music of the masters was inspired of God and they were devout men. As an example, Handel composed the music-set-to-scriptures for *Messiah* in only twenty-four days. As his servant, bringing him food, swung open the door Handel cried out, "I did think I did see all Heaven before me, and the great God Himself!"[5] Handel later tried to describe his experience by quoting from Paul in the New Testament saying, "Whether I was in the body or out of my body when I wrote it I know not."[6] It was an intensely spiritual experience.

Josef Haydn's music was criticized by the more stern members of his church for being too joyful. He replied, "Since God has given me a cheerful heart, He will forgive me for serving Him cheerfully."[7] This is reminiscent of the scriptures speaking of music as joyful praise. Haydn's work and faith were closely linked. He rose early in the mornings and prayed on his knees before beginning to compose.[8] "He always dressed up in his best clothes before commencing to compose, saying: 'I am now going to commune with God and I must be appropriately dressed.' "[9] At the last performance he attended of his glorious oratorio, "The Creation," the audience applauded enthusiastically. He lifted his hands toward heaven and said, "Not from me—from there, above, comes everything."[10]

We were given a very distorted picture of Mozart in the film *Amadeus.* His own words, in a letter to his father, tell us his true and spiritual feelings. "Papa must not worry, for God is ever before my eyes. I realize His omnipotence and I fear His anger; but I also recognize His love, His compassion, and His tenderness towards His creatures. He will never forsake His own. If it is according to His will, so let it be according to mine."[11] When his father showed concern about his marriage Mozart wrote him that "I found that I never prayed so earnestly, confessed and received communion so devoutly, as when by her side. It is the same with her. In a word, we are made for each other, and God, who orders all things and has accordingly ordained this also, will never forsake us."[12]

Beethoven had a complex character, was sometimes very gruff, but all his biographers agree that he was intensely spiritual. His relationship with God was deeply personal. He turned to God for comfort and wrote: "Therefore, calmly will I submit myself to all inconsistency and will place all my confidence in your eternal goodness, O God! My soul shall rejoice in Thee, immutable Being. Be my rock, my light, forever my trust!"[13] Beethoven composed many profound religious masterpieces and recognized that God was his source of inspiration.

Perhaps the most astonishing personal description of the process of composing comes from Brahms. In his own words he explained: "When I feel the urge [to compose] I begin by appealing directly to my Maker and I ask Him the three most important questions pertaining to our life in this world—whence, wherefore, whither? [Where did we come from, why are we here, and where are we going?] I immediately feel vibrations that thrill my whole being. . . . These are the Spirit illuminating the soul within. . . . Those vibrations assume the forms of distinct mental images, after I have formulated my desire and resolve in regard to what I want—namely, *to be inspired so that I can compose something that will uplift and benefit humanity—something of permanent value.*"[14]

Many other composers were deeply religious; they immersed themselves in the scriptures and prayed devoutly. Their magnificent works of music were truly inspired by God, and we need to have them in our homes to uplift and inspire us.

Our hymns are also a tremendous source of inspiration and guidance to us and our families. Our *Church Music Handbook* includes several quotes that bear repeating often to remind us just how potent our hymns and music are. "Music can set an atmosphere of worship which invites [the] spirit of revelation, of testimony. . . . The Spirit does not ratify speech nor confirm music which lacks spiritual substance" (Boyd K. Packer). "Music is truly the universal language, and when it is excellently expressed how deeply it moves our souls!" (David O. McKay). "Music is given of God to further his purposes. . . . Songs of praise to Deity help to sanctify and cleanse [our] souls" (Bruce R. McConkie). "If a child hears good music from the day of his birth, and learns to play it himself, he develops sensitivity, discipline and endurance. He gets a beautiful heart" (Shinichi Suzuki).[15]

The First Presidency, and many of the other General Authorities, have urged us to become familiar with our hymns and good music. "Music has boundless powers for moving families toward greater spirituality and devotion to the gospel. Latter-day Saints should fill their homes with the sound of worthy music."[16]

As women and mothers we sometimes feel overwhelmed by our many responsibilities: teach and care for our children, be good wives, keep our homes neat and clean, attend our meetings, magnify our Church callings, be active in our communities, write in our journals, attend the temple, do our family history, be a member-missionary, sometimes have to work outside the home, and so on. Is it possible to do *one more thing* to prepare our children spiritually for the years ahead—especially if we don't know anything about music? Yes! And it is the easiest! To enrich your life and your children's with good music is as simple as a tape recorder or a CD player and a few choice recordings.

In 1998 a new set of CD recordings became available that are designed specifically for babies. However, the music is electronically produced and some of the pieces are simplified, so the richness of real instruments is missed. But a psychologist claims that listening to good music increases an infant's creativity and intelligence.[17] Two of the four recordings are Mozart because his melodies are "pure and simple enough" for a baby's tender senses. The music should be played softly, as background, so the babies respond in a happy, positive way.[18] There are also many wonderful instrumental CDs for infants and children, including one called "Mozart for Mothers-to-Be."

As your children grow older, suitable selections are limitless, beginning with "Carnival of the Animals" (Saint-Saens), "Peter and the Wolf" (Prokofiev), "Jeux d'enfants" or "Children's Games" (Bizet), "Nursery Suite" (Elgar), "Surprise Symphony" (Haydn), and early Mozart and Mendelssohn. Whole symphonies will be too long for a child with a shorter attention span, so focus on one movement or section at a time. When the music becomes familiar, introduce the next part. It's just a matter of putting a disc on the player or popping in the tape.

How does one go about choosing good music and finding out what good music is? Talk to someone who knows. It could be a neighbor, a music store clerk, or a musician from the university. Many areas of the country have classical music radio stations you can turn on at home or in the car. Your local PBS television station often presents marvelous concerts to watch, as well as hear. Your child will become acquainted with all the musical instruments as the cameras pull in for close-ups, and they will learn to distinguish the distinctive sounds each of them makes. Communities and universities are a source of fine programs that are inexpensive. Libraries have records to lend and books to read about music and composers. The key is to listen, listen, listen! And even if they balk, instrumental music lessons are so very important for your child's growth.

Investigators into the psychology of music have concluded that:

"(1) Classical selections tend to gain more in pleasant affective value with repetition than do popular ones. (2) . . . Classical selections reach their affective height with later performances. (3) Compositions . . . of greatest musical aesthetic value show greatest gain in effective reaction with repetition."[19] The key, again, is to listen, listen, listen!

We began this chapter by speculating on what music might have been like in our premortal life—grand and glorious. Now let us think ahead to our postmortal life and speculate on the music of eternity in our Heavenly Father's kingdom. Can you imagine anything more magnificent than His harmonies of *praise* and *joy*? But for the time being we are here in the mortal world of choices—continual choices that can make our lives either mediocre or enriching and exalting. The choice is ours.

Just as we grow each time we read the scriptures over and over again, so it is with great music. "The real test of music comes from the heart of the composer. Bach said that the aim and final reason of all music should be nothing else but the glory of God and the refreshment of the spirit."[20] Let us make the small effort it takes to help our children blossom and prepare for the grand events to come.

NOTES

1. Boyd K. Packer, "Inspiring Music, Worthy Thoughts," *Ensign*, January 1974, p. 25; emphasis added.

2. "What Acid Rock Did to Petunias Shouldn't Happen to Our Teenagers," *The Denver Post*, June 21, 1970, as quoted in Hal Williams, "Dr. Reid Nibley on Acquiring a Taste for Classical Music," *BYU Today*, April 1980, p. 15.

3. Deborah Norville, "Music Hath Charms," in *Ladies' Home Journal*, November 1997, p. 158.

4. John Diamond, *Behavioral Kinesiology* (New York: Harper & Row, Publishers, 1994), pp. 96–98.

5. Patrick Kavanaugh, *The Spiritual Lives of Great Composers* (Nashville: Sparrow Press, 1996), p. 3.

6. Ibid., p. 5.

7. Ibid., p. 21.

8. Ibid.

9. Arthur M. Abell, *Talks with Great Composers* (New York: Carol Publishing Group, 1994), p. 66.

10. Kavanaugh, p. 23.

11. Ibid., p. 29.

12. Hans Mersmann, *Letters of Wolfgang Amadeus Mozart,* trans. M. M. Bozman (NY: Dover Publications, 1972), p. 205.

13. Kavanaugh, p. 38.

14. Abell, p. 5; emphasis added.

15. *Church Music Handbook* (Salt Lake City: The Church of Jesus Christ of Latter-day Saints, 1993), pp. 1, 2, 12, 13.

16. *Hymns,* "First Presidency Preface," p. x.

17. From an interview with James A. Incorvaia, director of the Reiss-Davis Child Study Center in Los Angeles, California, "Good Morning America," February 25, 1998, American Broadcasting Company.

18. See *Classical Baby: Mozart for Babies (Awake Time)* (Los Angeles: Kid Rhino, 1998), CD liner notes.

19. Williams, p. 14.

20. Reid Nibley, as quoted in ibid.

CHAPTER TWELVE

Hold Up Your Light
That It May Shine

"Therefore, hold up your light
that it may shine unto the world."
—3 NEPHI 18:24

by
Gwendolyn Wirthlin Cannon

When our nation was young and struggling for existence, a flag was conceived to symbolize all that was dear to those patriots and it unified their efforts in achieving nationhood. . . . Symbols are reminders-at-a-glance of what the group stands for and what its members are trying to achieve.

"Let your light so shine before men, that they may see your good works, and glorify your Father which is in heaven."

MATTHEW 5:16

*S*YMBOLS AND EMBLEMS HAVE ALWAYS been part of mankind's communications. They can take many forms—slogans, codes, visual images, or even an individual who inspires and motivates others. The banner held aloft in battle gave direction and courage to ancient warriors. The coats of arms of kings and queens have inspired their subjects for generations. When our nation was young and struggling for existence, a flag was conceived to symbolize all that was dear to those patriots and it unified their efforts in achieving nationhood. A country's flag is the emblem of a people and conjures up that which they love, respect, and value as citizens. Winston Churchill was the light that kept England from faltering during the dark days of World War II. He never considered defeat as a possibility, and he communicated this to his embattled nation.

Emblems and symbolic individuals embody the ideals of other groups as well. High schools, universities, and professional athletic teams have emblems that identify them and serve to focus their efforts on certain values. These symbols are reminders-at-a-glance of what the group stands for and what its members are trying to achieve.

When a new mission president presided over the Germany Frankfurt Mission the missionaries chose an emblem of the mission. They selected an eagle as the mission symbol. It helped them envision their efforts and symbolically extend their wings and soar to ever greater heights. Their slogan, taken from the Doctrine and Covenants, became a particular inspiration to them: "Therefore, O ye that embark in the service of God, see that ye serve him with all your

GWENDOLYN WIRTHLIN CANNON *lived eleven years in New York, over twenty-five years in England, and now resides in Salt Lake City. She received a doctorate in education from Teachers College at Columbia University, and has taught there and at the University of the City of New York and the University of London. Her most joyful teaching, however, has been in her home with her four children.*

heart, might, mind and strength, that ye may stand blameless before God at the last day" (D&C 4:2). This scripture became their byword. Each missionary memorized it, and they all repeated it as a group at mission conferences. It helped the elders and sisters to focus on what was truly important in their missionary efforts.

A symbol or a slogan can be equally important to families as reminders to each member of what their family stands for. It can prompt them to behave in a way that is consistent with their family's emblem and code. How important it is for children to understand that their actions reflect inner qualities of mind and spirit! A tangible symbol may help them to remember the goals and ideals of their families and motivate them to noble behavior. It can elicit the same loyalty, pride, and unity in family groups that it does for other organizations and did for warriors of old.

Children and parents can decide together what qualities their family wants to reflect. What are the most important characteristics that will help each member pattern his life after the Savior? In order to reflect these in determining a family symbol and slogan, a knowledge of Jesus Christ must be part of the preparation. He must be the role model. He said to the Nephite disciples: "Therefore, what manner of men ought ye to be? Verily I say unto you, even as I am" (3 Nephi 27:27). Instructing His Apostles at the Last Supper as He washed their feet, He counseled, "For I have given you an example, that ye should do as I have done to you" (John 13:15). And again He said, "Behold I am the light which ye shall hold up—that which ye have seen me do" (3 Nephi 18:24). He is remembered as the perfect example of love, patience, integrity, courage, and every quality that we should seek to emulate in our individual lives as well as in our families.

Read the scriptures and the stories about the Savior's healing the sick, comforting the lonely and the weak, raising the dead, loving and blessing little children. Note what qualities were evident in the way He lived His life. Determine what is appropriate for you to codify and serve as a guide for your family.

In deciding what to include, parents and children should choose what will benefit them individually and collectively. If compassion for one another is to be part of the symbol or slogan, for example, this must be important to all members of the family who are asked to live by it. If a family decides to be an example of goodness to friends and neighbors, perhaps they could choose a scripture that embodies this concept, such as, "For they were set to be a light unto the world, and to be the saviors of men" (D&C 103:9). A family for whom missionary work is an important goal might choose a scripture found in Matthew to serve as a guide and encompass not only following the Savior but also the responsibility of helping to convert others as well. "And he saith unto them, Follow me, and I will make you fishers of men" (Matthew 4:19). But it truly must be a family project and one in which each member contributes and feels that his or her suggestions are valued. Whatever symbol, emblem, code, or slogan is chosen, it must inspire and communicate to all who will be guided by its ideal.

The United States Arlington National Cemetery is the place where soldiers and patriots are buried. The religious faith of each person entombed there is represented by a symbol on the grave marker. The Star of David is on each Jewish headstone; the Latin cross identifies Roman Catholics, and the Protestant cross, the Protestants. It is interesting that the emblem that depicts the Latter-day Saints in this national shrine is the Angel Moroni. It immediately helps to identify those fallen heroes who are members of The Church of Jesus Christ of Latter-day Saints. A family symbol should have the same impact and significance on family members who understand the often complex meaning.

Symbols, emblems, codes, and slogans, to be internalized or to become part of a person's life, must be genuinely representative. Family symbols that are quickly chosen and ill-considered are hypocritical for everyone, but most of all for the children who look to their families for guidance on how to live a life. It is crucial for them to see that the primary people in their lives are truly living whatever code is chosen. It is the day-to-day observation of significant people living the principles preached and reflected in a family code that will validate those ideals for a child. Children must be aware of their parents' efforts to live in the light of the Savior. Surely they will recognize that we all fail at times, but they can also see the principle of repentance in action.

Extended family members also have an impact for good on a child's life. One loving grandfather uses short phrases to teach his grandchildren qualities he hopes they will remember. He tells them: "The hard is the good." "Finish that which you begin." "Seek wisdom in all your learning." These counsels are not scriptural, but each of his grandchildren has heard these short words of wisdom so often— and, better still, has seen their grandfather practice them—that they are memorized and repeated by the children and serve as reminders of a genuine individual whose example is a model for improving their own lives.

Joshua, a lively four-year-old, was determined that his older sister would not direct him. He said: "Shelly, you are not my boss. Do you know who my boss is? Mommy. Do you know who Mommy's boss is? Grandmother. Do you know who Grandmother's boss is? God!" This expressed in his mind the sequence of authority and put the grandmother in a position of supreme control, responsible only to God. Grandparents too must live by the light and reflect the code and symbol.

Children look to athletic heroes, popular music idols, movie and television personalities as glamour figures of the here-and-now and may consider them as role models. They fantasize on the excitement of such lives. However, when character and the other basic values are considered, ultimately it is the people whom they see every day doing simple things for them and each other who have the greatest influence. It is to those who have cared for and loved them that they will look when they are pursuing their own paths. As they establish their homes and families, children consider their parents and their parents' home as the standard for how things should be done. What a great responsibility this places on grandparents, parents, older siblings, and even valued friends!

How important it is for those in a position of power or influence to pattern their lives in such a way that they will exude only goodness and serve as a positive pattern for others to emulate! It is for the adults in a family to be that shining light that the Savior spoke of: "Let your light so shine before men, that they may see your good works, and glorify your Father which is in heaven" (Matthew 5:16).

Dr. Glenn I. Latham has said that he wanted people to remember the adage "I'd rather see a sermon anytime than hear one." He explained that "parents who fudge on their taxes, fib, tell half-truths and 'white lies' (whatever those are), and stretch the truth are modeling the very behaviors they deplore in their children—especially when those very behaviors are used by children on their parents."[1]

When I was thirty-two I faced the great loss of my husband, James, who died of polio. As I entered the corridor of the hospital that fateful night the sound of silence was dramatic, as previously I could hear the "whooshing" of the iron lung that helped him to breathe. I realized at that moment that he had been taken to the spirit world.

I had three small children at home and my initial reaction was panic. How would I ever manage without my eternal companion? At that moment the Spirit whispered peace. I knew exactly what I was to do and I was given the assurance that I could do it. My challenge was to explain to my young family the absence of their beloved father for this life. How could I help them understand and accept his death?

The principles of the gospel were my guide and my standard. The Savior had taught of life eternal and that ultimately we continue to exist in the hereafter with God the Father and Jesus Christ, if we are worthy. I gathered these precious children around me and we talked of death, of life hereafter, of where their father was, and I was able to assure them that he existed in another place, but that he was aware of us as a family and would seek to guide, inspire, and influence us even though he was not physically present. We spoke of him often, of the joys we had had as a family, of his patience and goodness, and of his many talents. At times we felt his presence. There were periods of grief. Tears were acceptable, but we explained that this was the adjustment of parting.

My children are now grown. We have talked of their father all of their lives, and they also have made him a part of the lives of *their* children. Several grandchildren have had the experience of feeling his influence, particularly as they sought confidence in a musical performance. Music was James's great gift. Kathy was four years old when her father died. I asked her what she remembered about that period of her life. She answered, "I felt great calm. I was not afraid." This was the blessing of the Holy Ghost. That great Spirit permeated our lives and sustained us.

Adults also need role models, heroes and heroines who influence their lives and give them light. As a young widow it was necessary for me to support my family. I found a role model, a heroine who influenced the decisions that I made at that time. She had walked the same path as I had, and had taken her family to the East to attend a university to pursue a graduate degree in her field. I never met my mentor but was always aware of her achievements and felt encouraged to strive for greater heights than I otherwise would have ever attempted. She provided the inspiration that gave me courage.

Positive role models are a primary need of children as they grow and develop, as well as for adults as they strive to live in a constructive manner. They see how those they love and respect incorporate positive values in their lives. As a family codifies these ideals, all members need to recognize them as they become part of the character of each.

Symbols, slogans, and individuals have motivated nations and people in past eras. They can serve to guide, direct, and inspire families today.

"Therefore, hold up your light that it may shine unto the world. Behold I am the light which ye shall hold up—that which ye have seen me do" (3 Nephi 18:24).

NOTES

1. Glenn I. Latham, *The Power of Positive Parenting* (Salt Lake City: Northwest Publishing, Inc., 1994), p. 237.

CHAPTER THIRTEEN

An Heir Apparent to the Kingdom

"Become as a little child."
—3 NEPHI 11:37

by
Shirley W. Thomas

This kind of effort [a child absorbed in working out a solution] however imperfect the outcome, can be seen as childlike and beautiful. One of the highly desirable childlike qualities we would do well to emulate is to really try.

•

"Go forward with faith."

PRESIDENT GORDON B. HINCKLEY

$\mathcal{N}$OT THE CUSTOMARY SORT OF GIFT associated with courtships, this thin black volume of T. S. Eliot verse had neither the glow and polish of a string of pearls nor the valued tradition of a fine watch. But it was precious. My husband, then an impoverished graduate student who had little else to offer but himself and his books, chose it for its message that he thought appropriate to our beginning a life together, and inside the front cover inscribed some lines he composed for me. As a cherished expression of his commitment to me and to our marriage, I treasured the book then and I do now.

It contains much of worth, but we have turned most often to the last page:

> We shall not cease from exploration
> And the end of all our exploring
> Will be to arrive where we started
> And know the place for the first time.
>
> A condition of complete simplicity
> (Costing not less than everything).[1]

We found in the lines of Eliot some echoes of truth—words that uphold our beliefs. Although we cannot be sure what he had in mind, when read from the perspective of the gospel T. S. Eliot's poem seems more fitted to our faith than he could have known.

Especially does the line "arrive where we started" support the sacred injunction "become as a little child" (3 Nephi 11:37). The

---

SHIRLEY W. THOMAS *and her husband, Robert, recently deceased, are the parents of three children and grandparents of eleven. She served with her husband when he presided over the Australia Melbourne Mission and with the Relief Society General Board for ten years, five of these as a counselor to Barbara B. Smith in the general presidency. She lives in Provo, Utah.*

scripture pointedly avoids directing us to *be* as a little child, but instead insists that we *become* as such, thereby partaking of the journey. The poem also emphasizes the journey with, "we shall not cease from exploration." Learning is an important part of the way to our "becoming." Our aim is for a studied state, an achieved understanding of what there is about a little child that makes him or her an heir apparent to the kingdom of God.

This is largely a schooling in appreciation, in recognizing divine, childlike attributes and then acknowledging and prizing and trying to emulate them. The text is the word of God received through scripture and the Apostles and prophets. Personal study and inspiration confirm the truth to our individual need. We who are adult in a child's world are both learner and teacher, helping the child to understand himself as we learn from him.

The last page of the gift book gave my husband and me some thoughtful moments as we began a life together and often since as we have turned back to it. Now we have come to another kind of last page in our marriage, as we near the end of our earthly exploration together. This may be a time to reflect on what we have come to know and appreciate.

When the Savior appeared to the multitude assembled at the Temple Bountiful, He very quickly began teaching them. It would seem to have been an exceptional teaching moment, for, along with the marvel of His presence, the people had just experienced hearing a voice as if it had come out of heaven, piercing to the very soul those that heard it and causing their hearts to burn. The Savior chose this time to tell them that He is the Christ, the God of Israel, and of the whole earth, slain for the sins of the world; that disputations are not of Him, nor of His gospel; and that to have part in His kingdom it will be necessary to repent and be baptized and become as a little child (see 3 Nephi 11).

He emphasized the necessity for becoming as a little child in two repeated verses. In 3 Nephi 11 verse 37 we read: "And again I say unto you, ye must repent, and become as a little child, and be baptized in my name." And the next verse says: "And again I say unto you . . . [and He reiterates the same thing]."

His emphasis gives strength to our determination to meet the conditions necessary to have a place in His kingdom. The prerequisites are clearly specified in the scriptures, and in the following passage from the Book of Mormon we are given a description of how this can come about, pointing to the fact that "teaching" is an important method for bringing about change. "Preach unto them repentance, and faith on the Lord Jesus Christ; teach them to humble themselves and to be meek and lowly in heart; teach them to withstand every temptation of the devil, with their faith on the Lord Jesus Christ. Teach them to never be weary of good works, but to be meek and lowly in heart; for such shall find rest to their souls" (Alma 37:33–34). Childlike attitudes such as humility, sincerity, and enthusiasm to do good can be fostered within a family without compromising other family activities and goals. A home that creates a healthy environment for the nurture of childlike attributes provides its tenants with a head start toward eternal salvation.

This begins to happen when we keep alive the good acts of children by approval and retelling. We have found that children, as they are growing up, love to hear about what they did when they were "little." And just as it is useful for parents to observe children in action, in the hope of learning more about what is childlike, so it is also valuable for children to be told the good things they did when they were very young. They grow in self-esteem when others approve their actions, and when they realize that even then they knew how to choose what was right. As young persons are growing into youth and teenage and encountering circumstances that challenge their self-worth or their established code of conduct, they can find strength in remembering who they are—who they were from the beginning. They can find that being that little child again, in principle, brings back the feeling of closeness to family, even to the Lord.

At first glance one incident that gets told over and over in our family has nothing of apparent significance to recommend it as a model of behavior, but as we analyze the intent of the heart we see it as an act of love. We were all overtired after a trip from Oregon that was fraught with the inconveniences and discomforts of travel in a car for hundreds of miles with two very small boys, but we were home, at last. We brought the youngest child, actually a new baby only a few weeks old, into the living room, where he lay in his bassinet, a little fretful. His older brother, himself but fourteen months old, in an overt expression of newfound friendship, located one of his "toys" from the bottom cupboard in the kitchen. With an arms-length, tiptoe-stretch he reached well above his head to drop a heavy, cast metal food grinder over the edge of the bassinet to his baby brother. Anyone could see there was danger in dropping a heavy piece of equipment where it could land on a nearly new baby, but there was also great compassion in what he did.

If we were to learn from this incident to "repent and become as a little child" it clearly would not be done in finding fault with this little boy. There was a need for teaching and explaining, but there was at least as great a need for seeing and appreciating the beautiful, the Christlike sharing of whatever he had with his brother who was in distress, the setting aside of his own fatigue and hunger to help another. If we are to place value on becoming as a little child, we will begin with seeing value in children; with helping a child feel good about himself by knowing that, although he may need to learn and to improve, he is, as a child of God, a very good person. We will want to help him continue doing what is, by nature, very good.

I remember that when this son was an infant, friends wanting to express their interest and their joy in our new baby, our first, would rhapsodize on how cuddly and cute he was, and some would ask, "Is he a good baby?"

I appreciated their asking, because it showed their interest and their concern for how we were getting along. I knew that "good" meant "Does your baby eat and sleep on schedule and cry only a little in between?"

Actually, many times our baby's food didn't agree with him, thus causing more hours of discontent than would have been ideal. But we had prayed and fasted and longed for this baby for four (what were for us) long years, and were so thankful for him. I couldn't think of him as anything but good. I still feel that way—that they come to us "good."

Another good-bad distinction for children is between the words *childish* and *childlike*. This difference may at some time have been arbitrary, but it now has wide acceptance, *childish* having a negative connotation of doing or being what is less mature than appropriate, and *childlike,* the positive one of resembling the purity of a little child. Using these favorable and unfavorable designations, we hardly need mention that we are seeking the childlike in our desire to please the Lord. It remains only for us then to exercise some charity in assigning those descriptions. For example, some behavior that might fairly be deemed childish when describing an experienced person could honestly be called childlike for one who is still learning. A child is seldom merely childish (if we are using this in a negative sense) until he gets beyond the age at which he could know better than he is doing. A child's attempt may be less than perfect, but if it is the best a child can do we would call that a childlike effort.

It has a great deal to do with "trying." One of the beautiful things of childhood is to see a child trying. He or she will be totally absorbed in finding the way to meet a challenge. This kind of effort, however imperfect the outcome, can be seen as childlike and beautiful. One of the highly desirable childlike qualities we would do well to emulate is to *really try*. I don't know how uncommon it truly is, but when someone gives an honest, all-out effort it is noteworthy.

Closely linked to this is sincerity, another childlike quality that has my respect. I love the look in the eyes of a little child who is earnest in what she is saying. She wants to be believed. Our daughter taught me about this.

When our children were small (and our house, too, by some measures), the two boys shared a bedroom while Angie, our only daughter, had a room of her own. Although her lot may have seemed desirable to some, she felt it a disadvantage, for she could lie in her bed at night hearing the two boys conversing in their room and us in ours, while she lay alone in her room having no one with whom to share her day. We did not think of this as a problem for her until one night when I went in to tell her goodnight and found her in tears. To my "What's wrong?" She explained: "It isn't fair! Cornel 'gots' Ryan, and you 'gots' Daddy, and I 'gots' nobody!"

To my regret, that complaint went unattended longer than it should have, because I failed to hear it as a serious problem to her. I had been so charmed by her expression of it that for a while I was *only* charmed. I heard it, repeated it to my husband and probably to the boys who, being older by a little, would also have thought her language "cute." But it wasn't a cute thing to her. She had a need. To her it was serious. It deserved a serious consideration for some solution.

She had at earlier times shown that same desire to be taken seriously. Once when she was three, she had come into my bedroom and, finding me praying by the side of the bed, had knelt beside me and whispered into my ear, "Ask Him for a baby."

She later remonstrated, "You know, if you would ask Heavenly Father, He would send us another baby."

I loved her faith; it was evidently greater than mine. It is so easy to dismiss children's ways as merely childish and charming when in fact they may be wise and discerning. We are told that "little children do have words given unto them many times, which confound the wise and the learned" (Alma 32:23). Knowing and believing that this is possible prepares us to be watchful and responsive.

Most of us remember occasions when a child could communicate to hearts in a way that an adult could not. Would there have been a better person to speak the heart of a people on that June day, and for nearly a century and a half since, than Joseph Smith's elder son, who at only six years of age, clinging to his father, cried, "My father, my father, why can't you stay with us? O, my father, what are the men going to do with you?" (D&C 122:6).

And sometimes the "speaking" is not in words, but yet expresses the feelings of others—of a stunned nation, as when the slain President John F. Kennedy's little son, John-John, gave a farewell salute as he stood at his father's flag-draped casket.

In both of these cases a child was able to avoid personal and political controversy to speak what was the essential tragedy of a young father being taken from his little boy and other family members. Another with more practiced oratory might have found blame, discoursed about fame, or filled in with fact and detail, but whatever else he might have done, it is doubtful that any could have touched more hearts than did these two young sons of their fallen fathers.

One of the most difficult challenges in our responsibilities with children lies in enjoying them fully—delighting in their imagination and talk, their wonder, their fancies, and even their silliness and fun, all that makes them children—while at the same time taking them seriously, learning from them and helping them to learn. Upon our success in this effort rests our eternal well-being. We recall the Lord's repeated, "And again . . . ye *must* . . . become as a little child" and that line ends with the words, "or you can in nowise inherit the kingdom of God" (3 Nephi 11:37, 38). Paramount to the process is recognizing the sanctity of every child's spirit.

Our family remembers two tricycle accounts, each revealing a child's spirit. There is something wonderful for a child in learning to ride a tricycle. (Conquering the bicycle also has a claim on childhood, but it requires another person to "hold" until the rider has enough momentum.) The trike, with its reliable three-point stability, can be ridden "solo" right from the start. This adds to the enterprise a certain sense of independence or "self" unknown to a "helped" learner. The few mechanics of motion involved can be quickly handled, leaving only the fun to be had. Still, to a little child, riding a tricycle can be more than play.

We hardly noticed when Ryan, our second son, started trying to ride, because he, typically, undertook a project independent of anyone's urging or invitation. I only remember that it happened not long after he taught himself to walk. The time, though, that will always stand in our memory, is the day he performed the feat. Ours was a pretty characteristic block in a pretty typical neighborhood, but for Ryan, circling it was an extraordinary challenge. He was trying to ride around the four sides—nonstop. It was hard. He had to build up his strength; cars kept parking in the way; "big kids" bothered him. There seemed always to be something working against him, until *finally* he made it all the way. And when he did, he and the tricycle became one. He was now master of the machine.

When it came time for dinner and I called him in to eat, he had his tricycle parked just in front of the porch step, but he did not plan to leave it. Savoring his success, he said resolutely, "I'll just eat my dinner right here" (that is, on the trike). We love to remember that day; it stands as an ensign to the power of determination in a little child, and the sweetness of triumph.

The other tricycle episode belongs to Ryan's little boy. His parents observed him one day as he was "living-out" Bible stories. Mastery of his big-wheel tricycle gave an added force to the power he felt through learning of biblical heroes. Their strength had become his; their commitment his own. And now, in the wonder of a vehicle he propelled, and over which he was in command, he could further the powers of goodness by becoming the Lord's agent. Brandishing a stick, which he explained was the jawbone of an ass (see Judges 15:16), he called out to neighbors and passersby that he rode "For God and Israel!" His commitment—even in play—to the army of Israel's God when he was yet a very little boy was a stirring witness of a vibrant spirit untrammeled by the world, intensely receptive, and warranting all the teaching his parents had given him.

Through the actual lives of little children we have been able to see some of the qualities that make them precious in the eyes of the Lord. When we are convinced that such things as meekness, loving to learn, caring about another's pain, and more, are required of any who would reside in a celestial world, we may learn to look as the Lord looks. Then, *sincerity* and *purity* and *radiance of spirit* will become words commonly used to describe all those who love and want to serve the Lord and to live eternally where He lives. As both learner and teacher we can endeavor to fit ourselves, and any within the reach of our influence, for life in that sacred realm.

There is one more grace the Lord has given to little children that makes a major difference for them. We might want to think of what it can mean to us. "For power is not given unto Satan to tempt little children until they begin to become accountable before me" (D&C 29:47), says the Lord. This is a blessing that anyone over the age of a child will not be given, for reasons we can understand in the light of our agency and need for growth; but to become as a little child we may want to think about what we can do to bring some measure of that blessing of the Lord to our aid *through* our agency and our growth.

The Lord assures that when He comes, Satan will no longer have power, and that is because of the righteousness of His people. But there is hope for that power of righteousness to be helpful in fending off Satan even now: "Pray always, that you may come off conqueror; yea, that you may conquer Satan, and that you may escape the hands of the servants of Satan" (D&C 10:5), and also, "Keep all the commandments and covenants by which ye are bound; and I will cause the heavens to shake for your good, and Satan shall tremble " (D&C 35:24).

If in our exploring, coming to "know the place for the first time" means to discover power in the purity of a little child, to see the beauty and sense the truth and the sanctity of soul that must become ours if we are to have place with our children, then yes, perhaps we have arrived back to a beginning, to a new realization of divine creation—a creation that must be our work with our own souls as we try to become as a child, and in our homes as we try to provide a climate to nurture those divine attributes in others. If "repenting" means ridding our lives of all that has no place with the childlike holiness we have seen, then maybe our poem described it well as a "condition of complete simplicity /(Costing not less than everything)."

For those who earnestly desire to become as a little child the way is clearly marked, the destination sure, and "a little child shall lead [us]" (Isaiah 11:6). We will have arrived when we have come to know what are the critical components of godliness that were the little child's as he came forth from God's presence and that both he and we must have to return.

While for me T. S. Eliot's "last-page" words are an interesting second witness to a gospel truth and will always be remembered as a part of an important and happy time, we know that for the life we have undertaken even the last page is not an end. And although we cannot see the next chapter heading we will, as our prophet has urged, "go forward with faith." We will continue to look for the godlike in every child we see, to foster the childlike in those we love, and hope for the time when we will find it in ourselves. Guiding us are words of another book, sure words: "Verily, I say unto you, that this is my doctrine, and whoso buildeth upon this buildeth upon my rock" (3 Nephi 11:39).

NOTES

1. T. S. Eliot, *Four Quartets* (New York: Harcourt Brace and Company, 1943), p. 39.

CHAPTER FOURTEEN

The Power of Heaven Among Them

"Then shall the power of heaven
come down among them, and I
also will be in the midst."
—3 NEPHI 21:25

by
Barbara B. Smith

We made Sunday dinner together a special event; this was our best talking time. In sharing experiences, triumphs, and trials around the table, we became a committee of nine to offer support, to give praise, or to enjoy together as appropriate.

"If these are the last days, and all things are to be gathered in one, and we are in truth the forerunners of the second coming of our Lord and Savior Jesus Christ, what a vast responsibility rests upon us!"

BRIGHAM YOUNG JR.

*T*HEN SHALL THE POWER OF HEAVEN come down among them, and I also will be in the midst" (3 Nephi 21:25). The implication of this pronouncement was seen with clarity on one occasion by a visitor to Salt Lake City. A distinguished businesswoman from the East, she had just been taken on a tour of many of the notable places of the city, returning, at last, to the Relief Society building, and she asked in a kind of unexpected candor, "Would you like to know what impressed me the most?"

Of course we were very interested.

"Two things," she said. "That incident at the creamery in Welfare Square was very moving." (This had to do with the compassionate concern of a supervisor for the handicapped worker.) "I can't conceive of someone being so kind. The other thing," she continued, "is this building. I have tried to imagine what it would be like to come to work every day in this building—the feeling, the way people treat one another, their attitude—I think it would be *just like heaven.*"

The years I served as Relief Society General President were, in so many ways, like heaven. The Relief Society building itself has a saintly air about it. Built with the donations of thousands of women, for many of whom giving was a sacrifice, it breathes the spirit of goodly women, of godly women—the spirit of Relief Society.

To coordinate our work with the other organizations and with priesthood leaders, we attended meetings in the Church Administration Building. Sitting in the offices or boardrooms, or even walking down the hallways of that building, you knew you were in the presence of the Spirit of the Lord. Nothing about being there was ordinary.

BARBARA B. SMITH is a lifelong resident of Salt Lake City, Utah, where she and her husband, Douglas, often enjoy gatherings of friends and loved ones. They are the parents of four daughters, Sandra, Lillian, Catherine, and Sherilyn, and three sons, Barton, Lowell, and Blaine. She served as Relief Society General President from 1974 to 1984.

One day we were on our way to a meeting, the three of us in the presidency, waiting for an elevator to the floor above, when the bell rang. The light flashed, the elevator stopped to discharge its passenger, and into our midst stepped President Spencer W. Kimball. Even though that was an everyday kind of thing, it didn't seem common to me.

When I was released I knew it was time, but still it was not easy for me to leave that assignment wherein every day had brought a new witness of the Lord's presence. But He has many ways of filling our lives with meaning and joy if we allow Him. The power of heaven was never intended to be felt only in the halls of some designated buildings. What better example of this than great-granddaughter Katlyn's third birthday? I called to wish her a happy day, and when she came to the phone I asked, "Can I sing you a song?"

Even hearing a three-year-old's drawled "Yes" is a source of incredible joy.

When I finished my "Happy Birthday to You," there was not even a pause before she replied, "Good morning to you, good morning to you. We're all in our places, with bright shining faces. Oh, this is the way to start a new day" (traditional morning song).

She didn't hesitate but continued singing until she had finished "I Am a Child of God."[1] And, truly, I knew that she was and that He *had* sent her here. And that in loving her we came closer to knowing Him. I couldn't think of a better or happier way to start the day.

Service in the Church teaches us a great deal about the power of heaven, how real and accessible it is. It gives us a perspective from which to value life, and experience in dealing compassionately with people. All of these can make our family life richer. It may be that the knowledge and experience gained through Church service has its finest application in our home, with our family.

I grew up "in the Church." I knew it was true—at first because my mother said it was, and later for reasons I could call my own. I was not always aware of when the transfers were taking place from her certainty to mine, but somewhere in the years of my childhood and youth with the help of the Primary, the Mutual, and Sunday School, the conversion came, and by the time I was in Mr. Lillywhite's seminary class there was little he asked about the gospel or Church history that was new and wasn't a distinct part of my belief.

But until I was married and had children I did *not* know the desire I would have, and that I still have, for my family to feel a heavenly presence in their lives. I remember as a young mother reading the 3 Nephi account of "angels descending out of heaven . . . ministering" to the little Nephite children" (3 Nephi 17:24). In my mind I could see them encircling those little ones, and I wished my children, our children, could have such an experience.

I soon learned that it is the province of those the Lord calls "His people" to have the power of heaven come down among them. The ministrations are usually not as visible as the blessings of the children in 3 Nephi (this vision may have been opened to us that we could know what is happening in the spirit realm though we do not see it), but if the ministering to the Lord's people is less visible to mortals, it is no less real. I wanted my family to partake of that goodness. I have searched for ways it could be so.

I always tried to have us do things together if we could. When I was a child, my mother was the Relief Society president (it seemed for years). There was always so much running around to do in our large ward, and she would put all of us children in our big black Packard and off we would go on her errands. She usually had us singing songs she ordinarily played on the piano. Maybe because my mother did it, and surely because I liked having my children close, we did things together. My children used to say, "When Mother receives a calling in the Church, we should all be set apart for it, because we all work together to fill it." This has become a pattern for our family that we still follow. When anyone has a project, all help. When one has a problem, we all pray.

We made Sunday dinner together a special event; this was our best talking time. In sharing experiences, triumphs, and trials around the table, we became a committee of nine to offer support, to give praise, or to enjoy together as appropriate. I think it was here that our oldest son first shared his personal witness that Joseph Smith was a prophet of God. He was a sophomore and felt that he should be able to bear a strong testimony of the truthfulness of the Church and of the prophet of God upon the earth. He wanted a witness so much, but it was a long time in coming. He prayed earnestly and often, but still it did not come. Then once, as he prayed, his being seemed filled with light, and he became light on his feet as if he were walking above the ground—three feet above. (I thought to myself of unseen angels circled about.) This feeling stayed with him a very long time, and its impact continues yet, as a beacon. His love of the Lord remains the first and foremost direction of his life. In much the way we share a calling from the Lord as a family, we have all shared the strength of this revelation, as a family.

In the Book of Mormon we learn that when His three-day stay with the Nephite people was coming to an end, the Savior told them they were to be His people. Remember that some of them had worked all night in order to be with Him during the day, and that their tears flowed when it was time for Him to go. They really loved Him and believed in Him so much that He told them: "So great faith have I never seen among all the Jews; wherefore I could not show unto them so great miracles, because of their unbelief" (3 Nephi 19:35). He said the Father had sent Him to them because of the covenant He had made with Jacob, they being a remnant of the house of Jacob. In leaving them, the Lord promised, "the powers of heaven shall be in the midst of this people; yea, even I will be in the midst of you" (3 Nephi 20:22).

Being the people of the Lord was realized in many ways for the Nephites. As long as they were faithful to His commandments, there "was no contention . . . the love of God . . . did dwell in the[ir] hearts . . . there could not be a happier people . . . they were in one, the children of Christ, and heirs to the kingdom of God. . . . the Lord did bless them in all their doings" (4 Nephi 1:15–18). The angels ministering to the children that had so awakened my desires was just one of the blessings they were receiving. But all of this was conditioned upon righteousness. And although the Nephites enjoyed so great a privilege—this special outpouring of the Lord's favor for nearly two centuries—it was finally lost to them. They were no longer worthy; they no longer had the blessings.

It was at this point in the history of the Nephites that I experienced a welling of compassion for Christ. Many times I had read these pages about the Nephites finally losing these blessings, and it had always seemed just as an inevitable result of their actions and had to be done. Then one time, as I was thinking of my family and the hopes I had for them, and of the Nephites falling away, I sensed a terrible personal loss for the Lord. These were His people! I wondered if He felt about them as I felt about my family. I thought of how He wept because His joy was full when they believed, and wept again when He prayed to the Father for each child one by one (see 3 Nephi 17:20–22). How familylike! I, of course, can't know what was in His heart, or how to equate His relationships to the family relationships we have. But His emotions were akin to those we feel. And as I read, it occurred to me that He wants His people to have the blessings as I want my family to have them, and as so many of those we know want their families to have them. True, there are many, many more of His, but His capacity to love has no limits.

One of the reasons why I thought the Lord might have this hope for His people was the responsibility He gave to the Gentiles. In time, He would offer them the "lost" blessings the Nephites had enjoyed, but with a difference. He promised, "If they will repent and hearken unto my words, and harden not their hearts, I will establish my church among them, and they shall come in unto the covenant" (3 Nephi 21:22). In some of the same words He used for the Nephites, He pronounced, "Then shall the power of heaven come down among them; and I also will be in the midst" (v. 25). But before He gave that blessing there was (in verse 24) this stipulation: "And then shall they assist my people that they may be gathered in, who are scattered upon all the face of the land."

He is allowing the Gentiles to come into the covenant, have the power of heaven in their midst, and even He will be there, *if* they will help gather His people in to receive the blessings. This is about children—the children of the covenant and our children. He wants His children to partake of the blessings, and so do we. As we assist in accomplishing His purposes, we become counted among His people.

Most of us know the sense of absence of someone who is missing at a family gathering. Maybe it's an "Uncle Walter" who never quite makes it to the reunions. President Benson used to speak of his hope and prayer that not one chair would be vacant when his family is gathered. It may not be one of our own children, but perhaps a brother or a cousin or an uncle, but your family isn't complete until all are gathered to fill their particular places. And if it happens to be a son or daughter, greater is the anguish.

I have an especially tender feeling about family gatherings, remembering as I write a time when our family became more complete, more whole. For a number of years one of our beloved daughters had been married, but she and her husband had been unable to have any children. She had always been faithful in the Church, and we continued to have happy times together as an extended family. But as happy as we were, still there was "something missing." Her family did not seem complete without a child. They applied for an adoption, and after an anxious time of waiting, on an appointed day she and her husband were called to go to pick up *their* baby girl. She seemed to have been waiting just for them, because, although the nurses reported her to be a bit unwell in the hospital, she settled into the loving arms of her new mother and never again exhibited another sign of that illness. Their home was supremely happy that year. Then came the culminating moment when their little daughter was sealed to them in the temple, to be theirs through all eternity. It was a time for family to gather together in joyous support to mark this most important event.

Life was good before, our family ties were close and true, but the joy, the sacred, holy feeling of being "gathered," of being whole, and one with the Lord, is a kind of fulfillment that must be called celestial and eternal. The happiness we felt that day, the radiance that accompanied that moment, are inexpressible in something as earth-bound as words. Our gratitude was truly without measure. There, in the sealing room, we believed we knew what it was to have the blessing of angels ministering. We felt encircled about in the powers of heaven.

Knowing the joy such events as this have brought into our family makes me the more anxious to help in the gathering of Israel, to bring the Lord's people home. About the gathering of Israel and our part in it, Elder Brigham Young Jr. said: "God requires at our hands a faithful performance of our duty. He has placed upon us a responsibility that few people have had since the world began. If these are the last days, and all things are to be gathered in one, and we are in truth the forerunners of the second coming of our Lord and Savior Jesus Christ, what a vast responsibility rests upon us! We cannot comprehend it unless we are inspired by the Spirit of God."[2]

Since the early days of the Restoration we have been taught of the necessity of the Lord's Spirit to be present when we are doing His work. In those days manifestations of the Spirit were often visible and unmistakable. It was as though there was to be no question but that the Lord was in the midst of His people. On the day of the dedication of the Kirtland Temple it "was filled with angels" and "the people of the neighborhood [saw] a bright light like a pillar of fire resting upon the temple."[3]

Prescindia Lathrop Huntington, a prominent woman in the early days of the Church, reported: "In Kirtland, we enjoyed many very great blessings, and often saw the power of God manifested. On one occasion I saw angels clothed in white walking upon the temple. It was during one of our monthly fast meetings, when the saints were in the temple worshipping. A little girl came to my door and in wonder called me out, exclaiming 'The meeting is on the top of the meeting house!' I went to the door, and there I saw on the temple angels clothed in white covering the roof from end to end. They seemed to be walking to and fro; they appeared and disappeared. [It was] The third time they appeared and disappeared before I realized that they were not mortal men. Each time in a moment they vanished, and their reappearance was the same. This was in broad daylight, in the afternoon. A number of the children in Kirtland saw the same."[4]

We know that the Lord is in our midst. We also know that, since we are His people, He has, as Elder Brigham Young Jr. pointed out, given us the responsibility to warn all nations of His imminent coming, that all who will may prepare to meet Him when He appears in clouds of glory. Elder Young said further, "If our message is like unto that which Noah declared . . . if the judgments of the Almighty God are to follow our testimonies to the people as the flood followed the testimony of Noah, then I say it is all-important that we be upon the watchtower."[5]

My husband and I had the remarkable opportunity to live in Hong Kong for over three years and have an actual part in this work of gathering. As a Seventy, my husband, Douglas, was called to be the Asia Area President and thus supervise the work of the Church there for a time. It was thrilling to see the Spirit spread its influence increasingly among those beautiful Saints and to see a temple (and since then another) erected in their midst. If we had known only the building of the Tokyo Temple or the Korean Temple we would have seen the hand of God manifest in a most powerful way to gather this people. Then to become aware of how the hand of the Lord made it possible to obtain the land in Hong Kong and the permissions needed for its construction—that required a series of events that the participants could only call miraculous.

It was a privilege for us, on occasion, to host President Gordon B. Hinckley, who has for decades worked among the members of the Church in Asia. It seemed to us that he has been the one the Lord chose to make the soil ready for the seeds of faith to be sown there. Indeed he has sown those early seeds and is now seeing their harvest! The Asian people love President Hinckley, and he, them. During the time we were in Hong Kong, President and Sister Hinckley celebrated their fiftieth wedding anniversary. Because Sister Hinckley wanted, more than any other celebration, to have their children come to the Orient and experience the joy that had always been hers in that part of the world, this is what they did. We were blessed to share some part of that time with them and to experience the great strength of that family. We felt the power of heaven and the Lord's presence as we were with them visiting the Saints.

Now we have returned to our home, and again our lives are enriched because of our service. My husband had experiences working closely with the Lord in that faraway land that have further magnified him and added to his spiritual reservoir. His wisdom to counsel and power to seal and bless are an ongoing strength to our children. We know that the promised heavenly presence is for homes as well as for congregations and so, also, is the responsibility to help gather the lost of the Lord. Our home is open to those we can find to help, and our hearts, too, are ready.

I pray for our family, for other families, for all of us as a people, that we will be ready for that supernal hour no man may know when the Lord will come in clouds of glory, bringing heaven with Him. I hope that we, with all of His faithful followers, might realize the opportunity we now have to be forerunners of this great event, and to unite in a far-reaching, soul-stretching, magnificent effort to prepare a people ready to receive Him. President Wilford Woodruff tried to prepare us for this spectacular time when he said: "The fig trees are leafing, the summer is nigh, the signs of heaven and earth all indicate the second coming of the Lord Jesus Christ, but who are really looking and preparing for the coming of the great Bridegroom? . . . He never will come until the revelations of God are fulfilled and a people are prepared for his coming."[6] The Lord's culminating promise to the worthy is the privilege to live eternally in His presence. This is the undying hope of all the faithful; but for now, before that day, we can try to create heavenly experiences with our families that will invite His power and Spirit into our homes. In this way we can prepare our children to know Him at His coming.

One experience with a lasting impact for our children was to sing of Christ's coming. The words of the song along with those spoken afterward by President Thomas S. Monson have given them a sweet remembrance of their grandmother's passing and a sure expectation of the Second Coming.

In company with other cousins they sang:

> I wonder when he comes again,
> Will herald angels sing?
> Will earth be white with drifted snow,
> Or will the world know Spring?
> I wonder if one star will shine
> Far brighter than the rest;
> Will daylight stay the whole night through?
> Will songbirds leave their nests?
> I'm sure he'll call his little ones
> Together round his knee,
> Because He said in days gone by,
> "Suffer them to come to me."
>
> I wonder, when he comes again,
> Will I be ready there
> To look upon his loving face
> And join with him in prayer?

Each day I'll try to do his will
And let my light so shine
That others seeing me may seek
For greater light divine.
Then, when that blessed day is here,
He'll love me and he'll say,
"You've served me well, my little child:
Come unto my arms to stay."
(Words and music: Mirla Greenwood Thayne, b. 1907.
Copyright © 1952 by Mirla Greenwood Thayne, Provo,
Utah. Renewed 1980. Used by permission).[7]

Then said President Monson: "We have just listened to angels sing. Children like these are angels that teach and prepare us to understand some of life's greatest lessons." He then assured those children that one day, if they were properly taught by their parents, they would be with their beloved grandmother again. Their song helped all feel a touch of heaven and of what earth will be like when our Savior comes again. President Monson's words comforted and consoled, but also taught of the important role children must play if both parents and children are to be ready when the Lord comes to gather the elect.

The singing of these young grandchildren was yet another kind of ministering of angels, as President Monson said. In their purity they blessed, and they taught that which was of heaven. In this they provided another witness of what the visitor to Salt Lake City learned through her tour; that to be among those who are living with purity the precepts the Savior provided as "the way," is to know, even now, heaven on earth. For the Lord has said, "I also will be in the midst."

NOTES

1. See *Children's Songbook,* pp. 2–3.
2. Brigham Young Jr., *Collected Discourses,* comp. Brian H. Stuy (Burbank: B.H.S. Publishing, 1988), 4.
3. *History of the Church,* 2:428.

4. Edward W. Tullidge, *The Women of Mormondom* (New York: Tullidge & Crandall, 1877), p. 207.

5. Brigham Young Jr., *Collected Discourses,* 4:157.

6. Wilford Woodruff, in *Journal of Discourses,* 18:111.

7. Mirla Greenwood Thayne, "When He Comes Again," *Children's Songbook,* pp. 82–83.

Index

Graciousness, 53
Grandparents, 131
Gratitude, 61–62, 100, 109, 151
Greed, 43
Guilt, 85

— H —

Handel, George Frederick, *Messiah,*
    121
Hand-in-glove analogy, 89
Happiness, 37–47, 59–69, 94,
    105–15, 111, 122, 151
Hate, 43
Haydn, Josef, 122
    "Surprise," 124
Health, 121
Heavenly Father. *See* Father in Heaven
Heavenly Mother. *See* Mother in
    Heaven
Heirs to the kingdom, 135–44
Heritage, 109–10
Heroes, 131–33
Hinckley, Bryant, 32–33
Hinckley, Caroline, 28–30
Hinckley, Christie, 33
Hinckley, Gordon B., on criticism, 52
    "Go forward with faith," 135
    in Hong Kong, 153
    on teaching children, 9
    on wayward children, 89–90
    on working mothers, 14
Hinckley, Rob, 28–30
Holidays, 107–8
Holland, Jeffrey R., on emulating the
    divine nature, 25, 28
    on prayer, 3
    "theological Twinkie," 3
Hollywood Bowl, 118
Holy Ghost, 5, 31, 62, 64, 133, 151,
    152
Home, influence of Book of Mormon
    on the, 17–18
    as a place of learning, 2–9
Hong Kong, 152–53
Hope, 32, 61
Humility, 62, 63
Humor, 62, 65

Huntington, Prescindia Lathrop, 152
Hymns, 123
Hypocrisy, 130

— I —

"I Am a Child of God," 147
Imagination, 141
Independence, 142
Independence Day, 107–8
Infertility, 151
Injustice, 40, 41
Intelligence, 119
Inverness, Scotland, 52–53
Isaiah, on peace, 46

— J —

Jack, Elaine, on complimenting chil-
    dren, 16
Jacob (Bible patriarch), 149
Jacob (son of Lehi), afflictions of, 83
Japan, 110
Jensen, Virginia, on mothers, 15
Jeremiah, on peace, 45
Jesus Christ, Atonement of, 30, 61,
    76, 89
    "be of good cheer," 61
    children of, 149
    "even as I am," 129
    graciousness of, 53
    had loving earthly parents, 13–14
    "His sun to rise on the evil," 44
    "I am the light," 129, 133
    "I love you," 95, 104
    joy and peace of, 38, 42
    kindness of, 94
    "let this cup pass from me," 43
    love of, 94
    "love your neighbor," 45
    and the Nephite Children, ix–xi,
        12, 51, 63, 148
    on peace, 38, 39
    "purified in me," 51
    as the Rock, 81, 82, 90
    on the Second Coming, 19–22,
        145, 151, 154
    on teaching, 2